MEDITATING
WITH MANDALAS

MEDITATING
WITH MANDALAS

52 NEW MANDALAS TO HELP YOU
GROW IN PEACE AND AWARENESS

DAVID FONTANA

DUNCAN BAIRD PUBLISHERS

LONDON

Meditating with Mandalas
David Fontana

First published in the United Kingdom and Ireland in 2005 by
Duncan Baird Publishers Ltd
Sixth Floor, Castle House
75-76 Wells Street
London W1T 3QH

Conceived, created and designed by Duncan Baird Publishers

Project Editor: Kirsten Chapman
Managing Designer: Dan Sturges
Designer: Clare Thorpe
Commissioned artwork: Sally Taylor at Artistpartners

British Library Cataloguing-in-Publication Data:
A CIP record for this book is available from the British Library

ISBN-10: 1-84483-054-3
ISBN-13: 9-781844-830541

1 3 5 7 9 10 8 6 4 2

Typeset in Mrs Eaves
Colour reproduction by Colourscan, Singapore
Printed in Singapore by Imago

"Mandalas are symbolic pictures used in meditation. Important in most eastern traditions, they take the meditator on a wordless journey into the mind's deepest mysteries.

The most basic of all mandalas is the circle, an intriguing symbol that has no beginning and no end ... It is the still centre of the turning world, the magic circle that defines and protects a sacred space within which one finds tranquility and peace.

It is the wheel of life, the symbol of ultimate perfection, the tunnel between this world and the world to come, the symbol of eternity."

CONTENTS

8 INTRODUCING
MANDALAS

SACRED PATTERNS

54 A Celtic Cross

56 Spirals

58 Thunderbird

60 Triskeles

62 A Hexagram

64 The Pilgrim's Maze

66 Perfect Symmetry

68 The Wheel of Truth

NATURE

70 A Bird's Nest

72 A Waterfall

74 Fire around the Lotus

76 The Green Man

78 An Octopus

80 Floating Lotus

82 Heart Lotus

84 Sun Lotus

86 Nature's Harmony

SELF AND ACCEPTANCE

88 Cranes among Clouds

90 The Flute Player

92 Yin Yang

94 The Flower of Self

96 The Star in the Well

98 The Salmon of Knowledge

100 Jewels

KINDNESS AND LOVE

102 Loving Kindness
104 Dolphins at Play
106 A Water Garden
108 Jacob's Ladder
110 Transformations
112 A Dove of Peace
114 Avalokiteshvara
116 The Dream Flag
118 The Rose of Pure Love
120 Islands

INNER STRENGTH

122 A Snowflake
124 Sailing the Storm
126 A Samurai Sword
128 Eternal Feminine
130 The Holy Grail
132 Confronting the Minotaur
134 Celtic Dragons

COSMOS

136 A Stained-glass Window
138 Time and the Universe
140 Dragon Energy
142 Sri Yantra
144 The World's Weather
146 Cause and Effect
148 The Endless Knot
150 Arches of the Heavens
152 A Pagoda
154 The World Tree
156 Palace of the Gods

158 Further Reading
159 Index
160 Picture Credits

Introducing Mandalas

MANDALAS ARE SYMBOLIC PICTURES USED IN MEDITATION.
IMPORTANT IN MOST EASTERN TRADITIONS, THEY TAKE THE
MEDITATOR ON A WORDLESS JOURNEY INTO THE MIND'S
DEEPEST MYSTERIES.

Mandalas are probably as old as humankind. In rudimentary form they appear in some of the earliest marks made by humans, and they are present again in some of the first scribbles of young children. They express through symbolism something innate in ourselves. Like all true symbols they arise from deep levels of the unconscious, and as such serve as keys which can take us into the mysterious recesses of our own minds.

The most basic of all mandalas is the circle, an intriguing symbol that has no beginning and no end and encloses a symmetrical area of space in such a way that each point on the circumference of that space is equidistant from the centre. It is the still centre of the turning world, the magic circle that defines and protects a sacred space within which one finds tranquillity and peace. It is

The circle of the mandala is a primal symbol for all that exists. It is the symbol of the sun, the giver of light, and of the full moon, the discloser of dark mysteries.

the wheel of life, the symbol of ultimate perfection, the tunnel between this world and the world to come, the symbol of eternity.

Not only is the circle the most basic of all mandalas, it is the form upon which all mandalas are based — the word "mandala" is in fact the Sanskrit word for "disk". Although the circle may contain other shapes within it, such as the square and the triangle, and sometimes may even be bounded on the outside by one or other of these shapes, the circle remains the primary feature of all mandalas. Without the circle, there is no mandala. But once the circle is drawn, then other symbols can be added to it. These more complex mandalas are major features of the sacred art of many spiritual traditions, particularly of Hinduism and Buddhism. At their most complete, these elaborate mandalas constitute symbolic pictures of the cosmos, replete either with the divine beings who represent or embody the cosmic forces behind existence, or with the geometrical shapes that signify these forces in more abstract form — the term "yantra" is sometimes used for these purely geometrical mandalas.

In the spiritual traditions, the mandala is frequently used as an aid to meditation. Because of its symbolic nature, the mandala when used in this way can help the mind not only to become focused and tranquil, but also to access progressively deeper levels of the unconscious, ultimately assisting the meditator to experience a mystical sense of oneness with the ultimate unity from which the cosmos in all its manifold forms arises.

THE MANDALA TRADITION

Although mandalas are particularly associated with the East, they have in fact been an important feature of Western traditions as well. In Christianity one of the best-known examples is the Celtic Cross, in which the centre of the circle is also the centre of the cross, whose four arms then extend beyond the circumference to symbolize, among other things, the four dimensions, the human form, and the link between the heavens above and the earth below (see page 54). In fact, the symbol probably predates Christianity. We sometimes see the cross contained fully within the circle, while at other times it is much smaller and takes the form of the rose, as in the "rosy cross" of the Rosicrucians (page 118). There are also echoes of the mandala in the halo that surrounds the head of Christ and the saints in Christian art.

In Islam, which forbids the portrayal of Allah or of Muhammad, geometrical shapes dominate sacred art, and a segment of the circle, the crescent, together with the full circle in the form of a star, represent the divine. The inverted half circle, the dome, represents the arch of the heavens and, by forming the roof of the mosque, allows the whole building to become a mandala, helping to turn the minds of the faithful toward Allah.

In Hinduism, Buddhism and Jainism, the three great traditions that originated in India, the mandala is an integral part of sacred art and a central feature of many meditational practices. The ground plan of the Hindu temple often takes the form of a mandala symbolizing the universe, with doors or gates at each of the cardinal points. Sometimes colours are associated with each of these points – yellow for the north, red for the east, black for the south and white for the west – while the centre, the point at which all four meet and from which all four arise, is green, the colour of creation. For the Jains and also for Hindus and Buddhists the lotus is sacred not only because its flower transcends the darkness of the water and of the mud where it has its roots, but also because its symmetrical petals make a perfect mandala. In Buddhism the mandala is an essential feature of the Tibetan tradition, in some of its more elaborate forms representing a mystical journey that takes the meditator from ignorance to enlightenment. In the West the circular maze, such as the one on the floor of Chartres Cathedral in northern France, is another representation of the symbolic journey from outer darkness to the sacred centre of the spirit, where the individual soul finds itself in the presence of the divine.

This traditional Tibetan mandala shows Vasudhara, the goddess of abundance and consort of the cosmic buddha, Vajrasattva. Around the outside of the mandala are rows of seated holy Buddhist figures.

MANDALAS AND MEDITATION

Meditation is a practice for calming the mind. Usually our minds are so dominated by what is going on around us or by our own mental chatter that we have little opportunity to experience the peaceful, tranquil state that is the natural condition of the mind. So habitual does this domination become that we take it for granted. If we are asked to stop thinking for one minute, most of us would be unable to do so. In a very real sense, our minds are not our own. They are so distracted first by one thing, then another, and so pulled this way and that by sensations, thoughts, memories and emotions and by the demands of the outer world that we have very little control over them. The result is that we live much of our waking lives in a state of tension; and when the mind becomes tense, so does the body. Mind and body are so closely linked that many of our physical ailments are a consequence, directly or indirectly, of what goes on inside our heads.

Meditation helps the mind to learn to become focused upon just one stimulus, and to cease to attend to all the distractions competing for our attention. The stimulus may be our breath'ng, or it may be a mantra (a sacred sound or phrase) or a mandala. If we use our breathing, we simply place our awareness upon the subtle sensation at the base of the nostrils as we breathe in

Why meditate?

Meditation is a path of self-discovery. We may think that we know ourselves, but in fact we live mostly in our conscious minds, and remain unaware of the depths of our unconscious and of the subtle spiritual dimension of our own being. By helping to still the train of thoughts that dominates the conscious mind, meditation opens us to the deeper mysteries of our inner selves.

The results of such a boost in mental power can be seen on an everyday level. By increasing our ability to concentrate, meditation can aid memory and make us more alert to the world around us. It also has potential physical benefits: it helps to relax the body and combat the effects of stress. There is evidence that for some people meditation may help to lower blood pressure, assist with pain management, and promote restful, restorative sleep. It may help to lift the spirits, and by relaxing the mind and body may even improve our physical appearance.

and out. If we use a mantra, we repeat it over and over to ourselves. And if we choose a mandala, we place our gaze softly and attentively upon the image. In each case, whenever our thoughts begin to stray, we bring them gently but firmly back to the point of focus. We do not force ourselves to stop thinking. Thoughts will inevitably arise, particularly when we are beginning to learn meditation or when we have had a busy or fretful day, but when they do so we simply refrain from attending to them. They are there, but we take no particular notice of them and do not allow them to take control of our minds.

Because vision has always been such an important part of human experience, the mandala has proved over the centuries to be a particularly helpful point of focus in meditation. Whatever form it takes, it can often hold our attention more effectively than non-visual stimuli. A mandala also has the added advantage that, provided it is a true mandala, its symbolic content will take us, without our having to make any special effort, into that inner world that lies at the heart of meditation.

STARTING MEDITATION

When you begin meditating with mandalas, even if you have practised meditation before, it is best to start with accessible designs, such as the ones contained in this book. The traditional, elaborate mandalas used in much of Tibetan Buddhism can and should be used only under detailed instructions from a lama who has himself been initiated into the spiritual practices that they represent. Use of these mandalas by the uninitiated is unlikely to do much good. The meditator can all too easily become distracted by the strength of the images and the vibrancy of the colours, and by the multitude of questions that they are likely to arouse in his or her mind. Like a secret code, to which the meditator does not have the key, the mandala will refuse to reveal its secrets. Instead, it is better to begin with something more simple, commencing if you wish with geometrical shapes.

Geometrical shapes have an archetypal force in that they are part of our inherited psyche, representing the patterns of the natural world within our minds. The mystery schools of ancient Greece, particularly that of Pythagoras, made a special study of geometry for this reason, and many of the sacred sites of the ancient world, such as the pyramids of Egypt and South America, and the stone circles of Western Europe, including Stonehenge, were constructed to conform to what is known as "sacred geometry", which reproduced through man-made objects the patterns upon which this world, the heavens and the cosmos itself were thought to have been constructed.

If you start with a mandala based on a geometrical shape such as a Celtic Cross (see page 54), you will find that early in your meditation a number of its symbolic meanings will arise unbidden in your mind. Without forcing it, simply allow this to happen. Note these meanings, without judgment, as they arise. Note how they seem to emerge of themselves from some deep level of your unconscious. But do not be tempted to linger over any one of them or to try to commit them to memory. You can ponder their significance after the meditation is over.

WORKING WITH THIS BOOK

Resist the temptation to flick through this book, glancing at one mandala after another without really taking them in. This doesn't mean that you must work with each of them before you can go on to the next. By all means look through the book – probably you will do so anyway – but keep in mind that you are not simply looking at pretty pictures. The mandalas are very much more than that. They each have a symbolic life of their own, and coming to know them will take time, just as it takes time to come to know new friends.

There are 52 mandalas in the book – enough for you to work with a new one each week of the year if you choose. But avoid thinking of the mandalas as forming a sequence from easy to difficult. Each mandala is complete in itself. There is no hierarchy between them. Some are based on traditional Tibetan mandalas while others are inspired by nature; others again are based on symbols found in various cultures, from Japan to Celtic Europe. When selecting a new mandala on which to meditate, you can do this on a purely visual basis, choosing the one that appeals to you most at that time. Alternatively, you might consider the mandalas' symbols: the step-by-step text alongside each mandala is ideal for anyone who feels daunted by the thought of approaching the images without specific guidance (see page 53).

Mandala meditation step by step

Meditation is at one and the same time disarmingly simple yet challengingly difficult. Simple because the basic principles are readily learned, but difficult because the mind stubbornly refuses to keep to them. The secret is patience and practice. Meditation is not learnt in a few days. But if you remain patient with yourself and practise regularly, progress will come.

1 Find a quiet room where you won't be disturbed. Sit cross-legged on a firm cushion that raises your bottom a little way above the floor or sit in an upright chair with your feet flat on the floor — whichever you find most comfortable.

2 Place the mandala you have chosen at eye level about an arm's length, or slightly more, in front of you. Start with a basic pattern such as a Celtic Cross (see page 54). If using a mandala that is not in this book, make sure that it is at least the same size as a page of this book. Straighten your back and rest your hands in your lap, fingers laced together and palms uppermost.

3 Now rest your gaze on the mandala but relax your eye muscles. If your eyes go into soft focus so that you can see two images of the mandala instead of one, no matter. This is better than straining your eyes. Blink only as often as necessary. Remain focused on the image. Do not be distracted by any thoughts that arise. If your attention wanders, bring it back each time to the mandala. Try not to think about the mandala. Simply look at it, steadily and evenly.

To begin with, practise for five minutes each day. If before five minutes are up you begin to feel disturbed in any way by the visual nature of the experience (see page 29), draw the meditation to a close. Remain always within the time limit in which you feel comfortable. As you become used to this form of meditation, you can extend this time limit, until ultimately you may be sitting for a full 20 or 30 minutes at each session. But never try to rush things or to push yourself too hard.

STILLING BODY AND MIND

The essence of meditation is stillness. Unless you are following various practices of the Jain tradition (one of the great spiritual traditions of India), which are performed while standing, meditation involves sitting on a cushion or on a chair and attempting to still both your body and your mind. Movement of any kind, apart from the gentle rise and fall of your breathing, disrupts the flow of meditation. This does not mean that if you are a beginner you must sit like a statue for hours on end. To begin with, five minutes may be quite long enough. But for these five minutes, try as far as is possible to remain still. Almost immediately, you will find that the body wants you to move. The body is used to controlling you rather than being controlled by you, and it will begin to try and distract you with the urge to shift your position, to scratch your face, to slump forward, to ease some small discomfort or other. Resist these distractions, not by a fierce effort of will but by gently moving your attention away from them. They are there, but they are unimportant.

Consider, too, the movement of your eyes. Whenever we look at an image, we tend to scan it continually from one point of focus to another. If the image is an enigmatic one, we scan it even more, restlessly seeking information to explain it to ourselves. Notice yourself doing this when you

Experiencing stillness

Do not become bored with the mandala. We live in a world of constant, instant gratification. Watch a television programme and notice how quickly each image changes, as if our attention span is so short that we cannot concentrate for more than a few seconds. Meditating on mandalas slows everything down. The frenetic pace of life becomes focused upon a still centre. The mandala is the exact opposite of the flickering, ever-changing television screen.

When you start meditating with mandalas, the novelty of this unusual practice may hold your attention for the first few sessions, but then the restless mind may begin to cast around for new stimuli. Do not allow your mind to distract you. Return to mandala meditation. Remember that this restlessness is simply a result of modern living. The whole purpose of meditation is to free ourselves from this, and to experience the stillness that is our real nature.

begin to meditate with mandalas, and how difficult it is to keep your eyes still. However, this is not the way to meditate. Take in the whole of the image initially, but having done so allow your eyes to come to rest on one point. Usually this is the point just above the centre, but there is no fixed rule about this. Do not strain your eyes. Allow them to slip into soft focus if you wish. Blink when you have to, but not more often than necessary. Notice how your eyes, as intent upon movement as your body, try to pull away from this point of focus in order to resume their scanning. Gently resist this attempt.

Just as the body is used to controlling you, so is the mind. Almost immediately you will find that thoughts start trying to intrude – thoughts about why you are meditating, about your daily life, about problems with work or with your relationships, about last summer's vacation or about next Christmas. As with bodily distractions, gently move your attention away from these thoughts. You cannot stop them arising, but you can stop them dominating your awareness. Like the body, the mind is used to controlling you, and resents having to relinquish this control during the period of meditation. But you cannot meditate if you are distracted by thoughts rather than relaxing into stillness.

Similarly, let go of emotions. Anger or resentment at some remembered confrontation with colleagues, fear at the prospect of an impending challenge, sexual desires, happiness at the thought of a new relationship or of some future event, will all, like the body and the mind, try to distract you. Such emotions can emerge without you even realizing it, but they can dominate your mind as much as thoughts. Become aware of them, then let them go.

In order to remain undistracted by the body, by thoughts and by emotions, you need to keep refocusing your attention on the mandala. Vision is one of our strongest senses, and if the vision is held steadily upon an image, this helps to calm the restlessness of body, mind and emotions.

THE ART OF SEEING

We are born with a wish to see meaning in the world, to make sense of experience. It is this wish that leads us as children to ask so many questions of the adults in our lives: "What is this for?" "What does this mean?" "How does this work?" "Why does this happen?" and so on. The search for meaning is further strengthened by our education. We are taught to look for answers, as if everything can be put into words.

However, we are born with a complementary ability to experience things just as they are, without questioning them or finding labels for them. A child can look at a painting and enjoy it for its patterns or colours and no other reason. Unfortunately, as our desire for meaning strengthens, this pure acceptance is educated out of us. This is one of the reasons why science has become exalted above the arts. Science is serious and purposeful, we are told, while art is at best a diversion, and at worst a rather frivolous waste of time.

Thus when we see a picture, even an abstract piece of modern art, we immediately seek its meaning, as if its meaning is something distinct and separate from the picture itself. And when we see a mandala, the same process applies. We want to know what it is trying to say, what it is for. This attempt to learn the secrets of the mandala by questioning it will only distance you from it. Instead, if it doesn't sound too fanciful, look at the mandala in the way that a small child would look at it, attracted by its shape and its colours, but without becoming lost in concepts about it.

As soon as you start meditating with mandalas, your mind will attempt to apply labels to what it is seeing. It will try to tell you the names of the shapes and the colours, to note resemblances between them and other objects, to establish preferences between this shape and that, between that colour and this. Note that this is happening, but do not become distracted by it. The mandala is already teaching you an important lesson. It is demonstrating that we have lost the art of pure seeing. We are so preoccupied with words, labels and concepts that we can no longer see things as they are in themselves. Bring your mind gently back to the pure art of seeing. Try to enter fully into the mandala meditation as a visual experience, no more and no less. The mandala will communicate with you wordlessly. And because pictures and images long predate language in our evolutionary history, it will communicate with you at a deep, primal level of the unconscious mind. The mandala's message has to do with being, not with knowing. Try not to pass judgment upon the mandala, either as something you like or as something you dislike. It just is, in the same way that you just are.

HOW MANDALAS WORK

Like all mandalas, the ones in this book are not artistic constructs, created to look colourful and attractive. Many successful visual artists, like successful poets and musicians, are open to a creative impulse that arises from deep levels of the unconscious. The artist expresses what is given to him or her, not what is put together by conscious thought. Ancient Greek sculptors, who produced some of the finest pieces in stone known to humankind, worked on the principle that hidden within the block of stone in front of them was the perfect form. Their task was simply to reveal it. If they allowed their own ideas, their own ego to intrude, then the finished piece was the work of man, not the work of the divine muses who inspired the creative spirit hidden within the stone. In the same way, the modern creative artist has to allow some inner impulse to take over from his or her own mind and express itself *through* the person, rather than *from* the person.

The mandalas in this book capture something of this artistic spirit. They are expressions of the deeper levels of consciousness that are common to us all. Thus when we contemplate them, they help us to access these deeper levels within ourselves. But do not expect too much of the mandalas. They cannot do the work of meditation for us. What they *can* do is provide us with the stimulus, a form of road map which, if we read it well, will guide us toward a level of understanding.

Looking at it like this, mandalas are both static and dynamic. Static in that they represent stillness, but dynamic in that implicit in that stillness there is the concept of movement — both from one feature of the mandala to another, and within the meditator. There is movement from the tensions of the body to a condition of physical relaxation; movement from the turmoil that is the habitual state of the mind to the tranquillity that is its real nature; and movement from the habitual superficial state of consciousness to something much deeper and wiser — movement in fact from the circumference of the circle into the heart that is its centre.

We use mandalas by preventing our analytical mind, the mind that governs our waking life, from intruding between us and the visual experience of the mandala. We sit in meditation, with the mandala in front of us, and allow ourselves to take it into our visual space. It as if this visual space, an expression of our consciousness, reaches out to embrace the mandala — or, if you prefer, as if we allow the visual space of the mandala to embrace our consciousness. Ultimately, there is no distinction between us and the mandala. It is outside ourselves, yet at the same time within the deepest recesses of our minds.

Becoming one with the mandala

In addition to shapes and colours, some mandalas – particularly those from the Tibetan Buddhist tradition – contain the figures of deities, such as the various Celestial buddhas. These beings are said to be personifications of the various energies that sustain creation and to exist both in their own right and as aspects of our own minds. Ultimately, it is said that there is no distinction between these energies and ourselves, for we are all aspects of the unity from which the world of appearances arises.

Traditionally, the meditator seeks to experience the truth of this by incorporating the mandala into his or her own self – this is sometimes referred to as "awakening the mandala within oneself". Becoming one with the mandala in this way is a very advanced practice, undertaken only under the guidance of an experienced meditation teacher. However, even the inexperienced meditator may increasingly feel a sense of strong identification with the mandala, as if it expresses something profound about the self.

This is why in true meditation, it is important to come to a mandala without preconceptions about its meaning. Like any visual art, the mandala means what it is, not what we can put into words. If the mandala were a language of words, then it would be expressed in writing. Pictures and symbols communicate with a space within ourselves that is far deeper than words, far more basic and primal, and therefore far closer to the creative essence from which all things arise.

WHAT MANDALAS REVEAL

One way of approaching the mandala is as a wise friend who knows us even better than we know ourselves. If we have a wise friend, we do not interrupt him or her, we do not deny what our friend is telling us, we do not come between ourselves and the things that he or she is trying to convey. When you sit in meditation before your mandala, it is important to have the same attitude. The mandala will help you to meditate only if you allow it to do so.

A great Zen master once said to his pupil that the reason the pupil could not make progress was that he had "a too wilful will". The pupil thought that he could not access the life-force within himself unless he "made it happen". The feeling that we must "make it happen" is endemic to our Western mind, ingrained in us by our education. The emphasis is always upon doing it for ourselves, upon learning for ourselves and assessing our own progress. This attitude is a great handicap in meditation.

Meditation is a process of opening our inner selves and allowing something to express itself that we did not know we possessed. Christianity puts it: "Be still and know that I am God." God, the Kingdom of Heaven, the life-force, the Divine spirit, call it what you will, is already within us. If it were not, we would not exist. Meditation is a process that allows the layer upon layer of conditioning acquired during our lives to be peeled away, so that this creative essence, the real expression of who we are, can reveal itself.

When you are meditating, contemplate the mandala and see what arises. However, if the sensations you are experiencing with a particular mandala disturb you, stop your meditation. The mandala you are working with may not be the right one for you at this time. Perhaps it is taking you too deep, too quickly. Perhaps it is unsuitable for your temperament. Sensitive spirits can sometimes be disturbed by a mandala that is too challenging or too abrupt. On the other hand, adventurous spirits may find that some mandalas are too neutral or too soporific. This is where a good meditation teacher can help: he or she can choose mandalas that are suited to your temperament. If you are working without a teacher, then this is an opportunity to look more closely at yourself. Notice to which mandalas you feel most drawn. Are you someone who seeks gentleness and calm, or an adventurous spirit who likes challenge, confrontation and change? You are who you are. No one temperament is better than another. Never force yourself into a category to which you do not belong. There will always be new mandalas that you can use. As you get used to this type of meditation, you may start to see mandalas in the world around you and elements of the world around you in mandalas.

PATTERNS IN NATURE

The mandala is a representation of a truth that lies all around us and deep inside ourselves. Thus nature, the creative life-force, is the ultimate mandala, a mandala that reveals itself moment by moment if we pause and allow ourselves to appreciate it. Nature is full of patterns and harmony: the light and shade cast by sunlight, the trees against the skyline, the dome of the heavens, the stones under our feet, the rain on the windowpane, the wind in the hills, the line of the seashore, the rhythm of the seasons, the ease of animals in movement or repose – everything speaks to us of the mandala of creation.

Look closely at nature and you will also see its "sacred geometry" (see page 17): the circles and angles, the lengths and the breadths, the heights and the depths. Look at the symmetry with which a flower arranges its petals, the delicate architecture of a leaf, the rounded curves of a pebble washed smooth by a river. See how nature arranges her colours, how each shade enhances and complements the shades around it. Experience how tactile nature is, with its rough and smooth surfaces and varied textures: the velvet feel of wet moss, the abrasive touch of a tree trunk, the contrasting surfaces of rock, the warmth of fire, the cool embrace of running water, the warm wind from the south and the chill wind from the north. Each of the four elements – earth, air, fire and

Take time to see the details of the world around you. The circles, symmetry and repeated patterns in nature are a visual reminder of the ultimate living mandala.

water – forms part of the mandala, as do the four dimensions of space (north, south, east and west) and the two dimensions of time (past and future).

Take every opportunity to meditate on the mandala of nature. Sit in the open when you can, allow your mind to cease attending to its mental chatter, and enter into wordless communication with nature. Become aware of nature without attaching concepts to what you see, without judging it or burdening it with the man-made labels that we attach to everything around us. Become aware that you too are a part of nature, an integral element of the mandala, the still centre around which nature arranges her enchantment.

Oneness with nature

We often forget that we are as much a part of nature as the trees and the flowers, the sky and the seashore. The four elements of earth are in our flesh and bones: air is in our lungs; water is in our blood; and there is fire in the warmth of our life-force. We thus form part of the mandala of nature. We are also a mandala ourselves, a five-pointed mandala that can stretch out to form a circle or a square, as in Leonardo da Vinci's famous depiction of the human body.

When you sit in meditation, rest your attention for a moment upon the mandala of your body, which, if you are on a cushion, forms a triangle, with your head as the apex, your legs as the base and your arms as the two sides. Become aware of the harmony and balance of the body.

If you are unable to go to nature, allow nature to come to you. Bring pot plants into the home and make a habit of sitting in front of them, allowing your consciousness to reach out and embrace them. Look closely at flowers, especially the composite ones that have a symmetrical arrangement of petals around a central "cushion". Hang paintings of woodlands and natural scenery on your walls and notice how they help you to achieve a state of rapt concentration as you sit before them. The mandala is always there before us if we choose to look.

THE SELF AND SELF-ACCEPTANCE

All meditation is an exercise in self-discovery. For much of the time we assume that we know ourselves, that we know who we are, but in reality much of our mind is unknown territory. We rarely explore the depths of our unconscious, or pause to ask about the meaning and purpose of our existence. We live on the surface of our lives, and in a very real sense are strangers even to ourselves.

The mandala is like a mirror that helps us to discover who we are. If the mandala is a suitable one, it is already a reflection of something deep inside ourselves, a reflection that does not judge or condemn, that does not flatter or deceive, that does not compare us with other people and find us better or worse, that simply reveals to us things as they are. When we stop to think about ourselves we become aware of all sorts of strengths and weaknesses, but the mandala is not interested in these. Like a mirror, it accepts all that it sees. It teaches us not to hide from ourselves. It teaches us to stop pretending that we are somebody we are not and to experience what it is to be ourselves rather than becoming lost in an artificial world of concepts, prejudices and needless hopes and fears about ourselves.

The self and enlightenment

The "self" is a rather vague term, but modern psychologists take it to refer both to the picture we have of ourselves — our self-consciousness and our self-image — and the unifying principle that makes us recognizable to ourselves and others as an individual. Buddhism insists that this "self" is subject to constant change, although our memories give us a sense of its continuity through the years.

The various demands made upon us from childhood onward can lead to the self becoming fragmented and subject to inconsistent behaviour and inner conflict. Meditation helps to re-integrate the self and to reveal a deeper aspect of our nature — usually called the "soul" or "spirit" — underlying the impermanent, changing self which we mistakenly believe is who we really are. The recognition of our true nature is sometimes referred to as "enlightenment", and this enlightenment is something that cannot be taught, only directly experienced.

A large part of human suffering arises from our inability to value ourselves. All too often the early, formative years of life have left us with a feeling of inadequacy, no matter how great our achievements. For many of these childhood years people may be more intent on pinpointing our failures and our inadequacies than on drawing attention to our successes. Meditation helps us to let go of some of these misconceptions. It teaches us that we are who we are, and that who we are is the place from which we must start.

Self-acceptance has nothing to do with ego, with developing an inflated view of ourselves, or with hiding from our weaknesses. It has to do with honesty and understanding. You may find that some mandalas in this book prove more helpful as mirrors than others. Feel free to choose between them, but do not reject a mandala simply because it does not seem to work for you initially. The self is a paradox in that it is at one and the same time both very complex and very simple. Like the mandala, it takes time to reveal its secrets.

KINDNESS

One of my Tibetan Buddhist meditation teachers used to teach that even if we felt we were able to do little to further our spiritual progress, we could and should always practise kindness. What he meant by this was that kindness is the foundation stone upon which all spiritual progress is built. An act of simple kindness can, in fact, be a perfect action, because it is complete in itself. Opening a window to release a trapped butterfly may seem a small thing to do, yet this is exactly what Christ or the Buddha would do in the same circumstances. The action is exactly what is required by the butterfly in that precise moment of time. Nothing needs to be added to it, and nothing taken from it. By becoming aware of this, and practising kindness in what seem to be the small things of life, we find that it becomes increasingly natural to practise kindness in what we may think of as the big things.

How can meditating on a mandala help to make us kinder people? The answer is simple. A mandala that expresses a deep sense of harmony communicates at an unspoken level the interconnectedness of all things, the value of peace and tranquillity, the natural and spontaneous way in which each element can support and enhance the existence of each of the other elements. Kindness is not an artificial quality grafted upon life, but something that arises of itself once we stop thinking of life as fragmented and individualistic, with each person concerned only for himself and with no thought for others. The mandala works by virtue of the relationship between each of its parts, which represent not just themselves but an integral aspect of the whole.

As with all mandala practice, avoid keeping thoughts such as these in mind once you enter meditation. If deliberate thought is there, then the process of meditation has already become an artificial exercise, driven by the conscious mind. The mandala must be allowed to speak to the unconscious. Often we become aware of its effect upon us only after the meditation is over, or when we have been working with it for some weeks or months. Harmony, tranquillity and kindness are natural states of the mind, and by allowing the mind to open to the mandala we rediscover these states, and they begin to influence and inform all our actions in both the inner and outer worlds.

LOVE

All the great spiritual traditions of the world teach that love is the essence of all things, that creation arises from and through love and is sustained by love. Those who have had mystical experiences say the same thing. They describe their individual self not only as expanding during the experience into the infinity of pure being, but as feeling the indescribable bliss of this creative, sustaining love. Ever afterwards their lives are changed by this glimpse of ultimate reality. Many of those who are resuscitated from clinical death speak of something similar, and once again the experience can be life-changing.

Love of this kind is very much more than romantic love. It is a unifying, life-enhancing love, which embraces all that is and which subsumes time and space and all that ever was and will be. Kindness is an expression of love in daily life, but love goes far beyond kindness, in that the experience of it can unify all opposites, reconcile all differences and end all strife and suffering. Mystics tell us that in the experience of this kind of love all mysteries are revealed, including the mysteries of life and death and the mystery of our own being.

All true mandalas — that is, all mandalas that are created through the intuitive wisdom of the unconscious rather than through the calculating knowledge of the conscious mind — are symbolic representations of love. Thus one does not choose one of these mandalas as specific to love. There is love in them all. At some point, one of the mandalas may appear to "choose" you, in that, with something of the intuition with which it was created, you become aware that it is communicating with you at a particularly deep level. If this is the case, then you may wish to use this mandala more frequently in your meditation than any other. This is perfectly acceptable. The mandalas are not here to be "worked through" in the way in which you would work through exercises in a textbook. They each communicate with you in their own way, and after practising with many of them you may find that you have a special relationship with one or other of them, and decide to use that one most often. However, it is worth continuing to work with those that seem to have less to say to you. It may take time for their communications to reveal themselves. Sometimes we learn more about the importance of love through our relationships with difficult people than we do through our friendships. The same can be true of mandalas. Each of those in this book has something to say about love, provided we give it the time and the space in which to say it.

Symbols of love

Although much used, the heart is in many ways the best symbol for love. Its shape forms an elongated circle. Harmonious and balanced, it resembles also the inverted triangle that is a symbol of the divine life-force streaming down from the heavens into the material world. Another excellent symbol for love is the rose, whose exquisite arrangement of petals forms a beautiful mandala. Both of these symbols of love can be used in mandala meditation, as can almost any flower and almost any leaf. Scallop shells with their delicate, converging lines are another deeply spiritual mandala.

The Earth itself, with its spherical shape, is also a mandala, and a wonderful symbol of love. The Earth sustains us and provides us with food and water and warmth. The Sun, which consumes its own being in the process of giving us life, is another perfect mandala and the ultimate symbol of self-sacrificing love.

COSMOS

These days, many of us live in towns and cities where light pollution prevents us from seeing the stars and the planets, and so we may rarely give a thought to the vastness of the cosmos in which we live. Even planet Earth seems to be smaller than a speck of dust compared to the vast expanse of this cosmos, and existing on that speck of dust our individual existence hardly seems to merit a mention. However, strange as it may seem, if we go into the desert where we are able to look up at the great bowl of the night sky, the sensation that arises is less one of insignificance than of being an essential part of the sublimity of space. The experience is one of majesty and grandeur, rather than of nothingness. This is because significance has nothing to do with size. The very fact of our existence as part of this vastness is significant in itself, and the mind reaches out spontaneously toward the limitlessness of which it is a part.

Mandalas carry a hint of this cosmic vastness. Some of the traditional Hindu and Tibetan Buddhist mandalas, such as the well-known Sri Yantra, are actually symbolic representations of the unfolding of existence, from the first small point to infinity, which contains everything yet remains empty. Meditating with mandalas can produce timeless moments of mind expansion, in which you seem to transcend the physical body and experience a state of

The Sri Yantra represents cosmic creation. The central point (*bindu*) symbolizes unity, the divine source.
The triangles are the union of Shiva and Shakti, the divine forces of male and female.

pure consciousness, freed from the constraints of the senses. Recollecting such timeless moments when the meditation is over, there comes a feeling that the mandala has provided a doorway into what is sometimes termed "cosmic consciousness", the realization that you are not only an integral and essential part of the cosmos, but that the cosmos is somehow contained within your own mind.

Meditation teachers always warn that one should never strive to achieve this realization. The very act of trying to attain it is a sure way to prevent it

Meditating with mysteries

There are far more mysteries in the cosmos than those discovered by astronomers. Space and time themselves, seemingly so familiar to us, are in reality completely unknown quantities. Space is the distance between things, yet what is distance? Time is a process of change, yet what is change? We are located in space, yet space is also located within us, in each atom of our bodies. We are located in time, yet there is no present moment. The more we ponder these questions, the more we realize that space and time, in fact the idea of the cosmos itself, are man-made concepts, formulated in an attempt to explain the inexplicable.

Meditating with a mandala, particularly one from the Hindu or Tibetan Buddhist traditions, can give us a sudden profound insight into the cosmos, an insight that does not solve its mysteries for us, yet perhaps helps us to grasp something of their awesome immensity.

from happening. Like everything else of value in meditation it arises, if it will, of itself. Resist the temptation of trying to see things in the mandala, to make sense of its imagery. And resist the temptation to scan the mandala, eyes flicking from one point to another. Remember that in all mandala meditation it is essential to keep the eyes fixed on one point, usually at or just above the centre of the mandala. And remember too that in meditation you do not have to do things for yourself, to strive for certain effects. All that is needed is that you keep the mind as still as possible, undistracted by thoughts or emotions, or by physical sensations. You did not create the cosmos, and you cannot expect it to reveal itself to you through any efforts of your own.

MAKING YOUR OWN MANDALA

The great Swiss psychiatrist Carl Jung made an extensive study of mandalas, detecting in them a range of potential symbolic meanings. He noticed that as his clients progressed in the course of psychotherapy they spontaneously began to create their own mandalas. For Jung, mandalas were intimately associated with both psychological and spiritual health. When he built a house for himself at Bollingen, overlooking Lake Geneva, he constructed it in mandala form. You, too, may wish at some stage to construct your own mandala.

If you do decide to create a mandala, there are certain guidelines to keep in mind. Firstly, it must not be the result of conscious effort. If you construct a mandala by thinking about it, you will produce something that may look attractive but will essentially be an artificial exercise. The mandala should arise from your unconscious, as if given to you by some power greater than yourself. It may be that your mandala will appear in your mind spontaneously during a meditation session. Or you may wish to sit before a blank sheet of paper, empty your mind of thoughts, and just draw whatever

Avoid preconceptions

Only attempt to create your own mandala if you feel drawn to do so. It is not a test of your progress in meditation. If you do wish to create one, work on a sheet of paper of at least A4 size, and equip yourself with several coloured pencils – red, green, yellow and blue as a minimum. Put yourself in a meditative frame of mind. Try to drop any preconceptions of how your mandala should look. Work freehand. You can always carry out minor corrections later if you wish.

Start with a geometrical shape, whichever one comes to mind, then add colours and other shapes as they come to mind. The whole process should be creative and spontaneous, arising from the unconscious rather than from conscious deliberation. Don't *try* for balance. Draw what comes. The results may surprise you.

Resist the temptation to destroy your mandala if you dislike it. Put it aside, and perhaps try working with it again when the mood takes you.

comes to mind. It may take several attempts before something arrives that seems to speak directly to you.

Secondly, the mandala is not simply a drawing inside a circle or square. It should have a recognizable symmetry and convey a sense of balance and harmony. It should represent something beyond its immediate appearance, something that you feel will reveal itself little by little as you meditate on it.

Thirdly, never try to force the pace. If something meaningful does not arise, no matter. Don't see this as failure. You may prefer to stay with the mandalas created by others. Traditional mandalas have stood the test of time, meaning that they represent something profound and enduring in ourselves.

Fourthly, don't be afraid to put your mandala to one side if you become dissatisfied with it. Don't allow yourself to become attached to it just because it's your own. It is simply there to help you, and if it ceases to do so, be prepared to let it go.

Instead of creating your own mandala, you may feel moved to adapt one of those in this book. Their purpose is to help you to experiment with meditation. But once again, be sure to work from your unconscious mind rather than from your normal, analytical consciousness. Don't be tempted to alter a mandala simply to make it look more attractive. Mandalas are things of beauty, but their beauty is an expression of their underlying meaning and harmony. They should never be seen simply as decorative objects. And don't be tempted to try altering one of the mandalas that come from the great spiritual traditions: they already have their own timeless wisdom.

SYMBOLISM

Carl Jung noted that the mandalas his patients produced tended to develop more harmony and meaning as their treatment progressed. In his view the centre of the mandala can be seen as symbolizing the self, the total personality, while the periphery represents everything that belongs to the self — that is, the opposing elements that make up the total personality. For Jung, psychological health is always a matter of balancing these elements within oneself, so that the personality experiences an inner harmony and can express all its natural energies in an appropriate and effective way.

As you progress in meditation, you may find that the symbolism in the various mandalas with which you are working becomes increasingly apparent. Some symbols carry an almost universal meaning, while others are personal to yourself. As you meditate, do not make a particular attempt to identify symbolism in the mandala, or to speculate as to the meaning intended by the creator of the mandala. Symbols work best if they are received initially at an unconscious level and their meaning is allowed to arise spontaneously into conscious awareness. Nevertheless, some prior knowledge of symbols that carry universal meaning can be helpful to the more advanced meditator.

Buddhist mandalas traditionally use four basic colours – white, yellow, red and green – that represent the four directions, as well as the four elements of the human personality analogous to those identified by the psychologist Hans Eysenck (extroversion, introversion, stability and neuroticism). White also symbolizes purity, while yellow symbolizes the divine principle expressed in matter. Red represents energy and the life-force, and green the natural world. Subsequently, blue has been used to symbolize infinity and peace, while purple and violet both stand for mysticism and spiritual attainment.

Shapes also carry symbolic meaning. The cross represents the descent of the divine life-force into matter. The circle symbolizes completion, movement, perfection, with no end and no beginning. The square stands for balance, safety and the four directions. The upward-pointing triangle symbolizes man's ascent to the divine, while the downward-pointing triangle represents the divine reaching down to man. Jung considered that the relationship between the circle and the square was of particular symbolic importance to the meditator. He referred frequently in his writings to "squaring the circle", which we can take to mean the act of reconciling the square, symbolizing consciousness and the outer material world, with the circle, symbolizing the unconscious and the inner spiritual world. Such reconciliation makes conscious the mysteries hidden within the unconscious.

The 52 mandalas in this book reflect the traditional symbolism of various cultures around the world – but with a degree of imaginative invention, too. Meditators are advised to follow the approaches I have described in this introduction. But initially you might like to acquaint yourself with some of the intuitive symbolic thinking behind these new mandalas, as described in the step-by-step guidelines accompanying each one. For advice on how to use these, see page 53.

CONTINUING THE PRACTICE

It is for you to decide how to continue with mandala meditation. You may wish to include it as part of another meditation programme – for example, one that focuses upon breathing – and use it only from time to time. Alternatively, you may choose to use mandala meditation as your main programme. Either way, to make progress in meditation try to sit each day, either morning or evening or both, for at least 20 to 30 minutes. Build up to this slowly, never trying to force the pace. If possible, try to sit at the same time each day, and establish, if you can, a special place — such as the corner of a room — in which to sit, with a cushion or a chair that you use only for meditation. Wear something light and comfortable, such as a tracksuit or a dressing gown, preferably in a tranquil colour that will harmonize with the tranquillity of your meditation.

Seeking the truth

Dogen, the founder of the Soto Zen tradition, taught that one does not meditate in order to become a buddha, but because meditation is what buddhas do. In other words, the very act of sitting in meditation is the act of a buddha. Dogen is referring, of course, to genuine meditation, not simply to sitting lost in thought. But his teaching makes clear that meditation is not only for advanced practitioners. It belongs to us all, as it is the natural state of the mind when the mind becomes still. Meditation does not add something to the mind that is not already there. It strips away the obscurations that prevent the mind from experiencing its own true nature.

This profound truth is a great incentive to continue practising. In meditation we are re-discovering insights into ourselves that have always been there but are now forgotten — also insights that not only confirm our humanity but that reveal that we are spiritual beings, expressions of the unifying creative force from which all things, both seen and unseen, arise.

If you have created your own mandala, use it if it feels right, but be ready to create a new mandala for yourself if you feel the urge. Notice how the new mandala differs from the old. Meditation is not a form of psychotherapy such as that used by Carl Jung with his patients, but nevertheless you may be aware of subtle developments in your mandala. Don't try to analyze these too closely, nor consciously to "improve" your mandala in an effort to demonstrate that you are making progress. However, note that these differences in shapes and colours may reflect a growing state of inner harmony and balance.

If after persevering with meditation for some time it seems to bring no benefits, don't be discouraged. Changes may have taken place at an unconscious level. And many meditators, although they may stop practising at certain points in their lives, come back to it later. If you find that you have no wish to continue with meditation for the present, put this book to one side, but try not to forget it completely. Like everything to do with meditation, it is here to help you. To adapt the words of one of the greatest of all teachers (Jesus Christ), meditation is made for man and not man for meditation. It remains, like a wise and loyal friend, ever ready to come to our assistance when we need it, such as periods of stress or uncertainty, whenever we need to find the peace that lies always deep within ourselves.

In the Zen garden one of the aims is to capture the essence of a natural object, just as meditation allows us to experience that quiet, tranquil state at the core of our being.

Mandalas for Meditation

HOW TO USE THE GUIDELINES

The step-by-step guidelines alongside each meditation are intended

to introduce the beginner to some of the thinking behind the image

and to open the mind to some of its possible symbolic resonances.

As your meditative practice develops, these guidelines can be left

behind, so the mandalas are allowed to work at an increasingly more

intuitive and personal symbolic level. Although the mandalas are

organized theme by theme for ease of reference, your experience of

any of the mandalas is very much your own, and the thematic structure

should not be taken as definitive. All the mandalas are, at the deepest

level, a reflection of the self, the cosmos and the love

that binds everything together.

A Celtic Cross

THE CELTIC CROSS COMBINES TWO POWERFUL SYMBOLS: THE

CIRCLE, SUGGESTING INFINITY OR THE ETERNAL; AND THE

CROSS, SUGGESTING THE WORLD OF PHYSICAL FORMS. IN

ANCIENT TIMES THE IMAGE PROBABLY DENOTED CREATIVITY.

1 Look at the two basic forms: in essence, the circle suggests the feminine principle and the cross the masculine principle. The interplay of both is all creation.

2 Now move to a higher level of symbolism, seeing the circle as eternity and the cross as the created world. The arms of the cross represent the points of the compass and the four elements.

3 See the fifth element, spirit, as the circle, which also is the circle of life and the endless path of knowledge, all fused into an all-embracing cosmic harmony. Let this enter your mind like water filling a well.

If you want to understand the Creator,
seek to understand created things.

ST COLUMBANUS (C. 543–615)

Spirals

THE CELTS AND OTHER ANCIENT PEOPLES ARE THOUGHT TO
HAVE USED SPIRALS AS SYMBOLS OF THE SUN, SOURCE OF ALL
LIFE. THIS MANDALA REFLECTS THE UNDYING ENERGY OF THE
UNIVERSE – AS WELL AS THE PROGRESS OF THE SOUL.

1 First, see the spirals of the mandala as the dance of divine solar energy, powering all life and all that exists.

2 Now think of the spirals as your voyage to enlightenment. Progress toward the still centre at the heart of the self, slowly but surely getting closer. The harmony of this mandala evolves out of our essential goodness as we seek and find the truth.

3 In your mind, fuse these meanings together – the cosmic and the personal. Perceive the different spirals as merging into one image that represents the growth of nature and the growth of the soul, the flow of the cosmos and the flow of your own understanding, the creation and dissolution of the world and your own self within the world.

The Sun, hearth of affection and of life,
pours ardent love on the delighted Earth.

ARTHUR RIMBAUD (1854–1891)

Thunderbird

FOR NATIVE AMERICANS THE GREAT SPIRIT MANIFESTED
HIMSELF IN VARIOUS NATURAL FORMS, INCLUDING
THUNDERBIRD, GUARDIAN OF THE SKY, WHO WAS ENGAGED IN
ENDLESS BATTLE WITH THE SERPENTS OF THE UNDERWORLD.

1 Look at the bird in the centre of this mandala: Thunderbird. This can be seen as symbolizing the source of active good in the world, the energy that nourishes our virtues and keeps us alert to all moral dangers.

2 Now contemplate the spiral pattern that surrounds Thunderbird — representing the endless flowering of creation within the transparency of pure mind.

3 Take the bird's energies into your mind as a totem of your spiritual self-knowledge. Whatever your beliefs, this powerful image of the natural world, a bird at home in the storm, can help you to affirm your purpose.

Listen to the voice of nature,
for it holds treasures for us all.

HURON SAYING

Triskeles

IN ITS THREE LINKED SPIRALS, THE TRISKELE IS TYPICALLY

CELTIC. IT DENOTES THE SUN, THE AFTERLIFE AND

REINCARNATION. THIS MANDALA MEDITATION MAY ALSO

GENERATE BENEFICIAL ENERGIES IF YOU ARE PREGNANT.

1 Trace in your mind the continuous line of the triple spiral. This, like the endless knot (see page 149), suggests the endless repetition of life's cycles — a life-force restlessly manifesting itself, and the eternity that is implied by such a perspective.

2 Now see this life-force framed within the context of eternal spirit — as reflected in the perfect outer circle of the mandala.

3 Take into your mind this perfect balance of being and becoming, of eternal emptiness and vibrant creation, and let these harmonies radiate through your mind, into body, heart and bloodstream. You are endlessly creative, even as you abide in the stillness of the spirit.

Every creation
originates in love.

LU XUN (1881–1936)

A Hexagram

THE HEXAGRAM IS A PAIR OF INTERLOCKING TRIANGLES,

REPRESENTING UNITY IN DUALITY. IN JUDAISM THE SYMBOL IS

KNOWN AS THE STAR OF DAVID, AND IS ALSO ASSOCIATED WITH

SOLOMON. HEXAGRAMS ALSO APPEAR IN HINDU MANDALAS.

1 Identify the upward-pointing triangle, which is masculine and symbolizes fire; and the downward-pointing one, which is feminine and denotes water.

2 Observe the upper half of the upward triangle, with the base of the downward triangle crossing through it: this is the symbol for air. Then observe the lower half of the downward triangle, again with a horizontal bar across it: this is the symbol for earth. The mandala, then, contains all four elements.

3 Take the mandala as a whole into your mind. As you do so, you are absorbing all the elements, all creation. The fifth element, spirit, denoted by the outer circle, is the medium through which your inner life unfolds.

Those who worship Me with devotion,
they are in Me and I am in them.

THE BHAGAVAD GITA (C. 500 BC)

The Pilgrim's Maze

THE LABYRINTH WAS ONCE A SYMBOL OF MORAL CONFUSION,

BUT IN THE MIDDLE AGES CHRISTIANS BEGAN TO SEE IT AS

THE TRUE WAY OF BELIEF. THIS MANDALA IS BASED ON THE

MAZE ON THE FLOOR OF CHARTRES CATHEDRAL, FRANCE.

1 Follow the labyrinth from its entrance (at the bottom) all the way to the floral device at its centre. You should not lose your way, because the labyrinth is unicursal — that is, it has no junctions. But if you forget where you are, go back to the start and try again.

2 As you get closer to the centre, imagine travelling deeper and deeper into the self. The labyrinth is your physical incarnation, the life you lead on Earth; and, at the same time, it is the challenges that you face in following your spiritual destiny.

3 Once you reach the centre, view it as a tunnel that leads down into the page. Step into this tunnel. For many the labyrinth continues, but for you the path is now straight — as long as you keep the purity of heart that your pilgrimage has brought you.

*The perfect way is only difficult
for those who pick and choose.*

SENG-TS'AN (C. 520–606)

Perfect Symmetry

THIS MANDALA, LIKE THE SRI YANTRA (SEE PAGE 40), CAN
HELP THE MEDITATOR TO GO BACK SYMBOLICALLY TO THE
MOMENT OF CREATION. IT REMINDS US THAT THERE IS NO
FUNDAMENTAL DIFFERENCE BETWEEN SUBJECT AND OBJECT.

1 Appreciate the different shapes of the mandala, starting with the triangular segments, denoting the physical world, and turning next to the concentric circles, suggesting all-embracing spiritual perfection. Note also the "tear splashes" around the edges – suggestive of joy and sorrow.

2 Look at the criss-crossing lines, going off in different directions. These represent the male and female principles that give rise, in their interplay, to creation. The central cluster of circles is the divine source of all life, pulsing with energy, as if the sun had been squeezed to the size of a button.

3 Let all the energies of the mandala float deeper and deeper into your consciousness, until your mind achieves a perfect and peaceful resonance.

Everything in the universe is within you.
Ask for everything from yourself.

JALIL AL-DIN RUMI (1207–1273)

The Wheel of Truth

THE WHEEL IN THIS MANDALA, BASED ON A TIBETAN ORIGINAL,
SYMBOLIZES THE TEACHINGS OF BUDDHISM, INCLUDING THE
GOALS OF ABSOLUTE SELFLESSNESS AND TRUE PERCEPTION.
ITS CENTRAL SPIRALS DENOTE WISDOM AND COMPASSION.

1 Look at the square frame in which the mandala sits — representing the solidity and density of the material world.

2 Now turn to the wheel itself. The hub is a double yin yang symbol, around which are circles showing the steps toward enlightenment. The wheel's eight spokes symbolize the Buddha's Eightfold Path: right speech, right action, right livelihood, right effort, right mindfulness, right concentration, right view and right thought.

3 Look at the stylized lotus designs on the rim of the wheel, reflecting the pure heart that is filled with love and wisdom. Absorb the wheel into yourself as a guide and commitment to purity and wholeness.

*Happiness is when what you think, what you say
and what you do are in harmony.*

MOHANDAS K. GANDHI (1869–1948)

A Bird's Nest

MANDALAS BASED WHOLLY ON THE NATURAL WORLD HAVE
A UNIVERSAL DIMENSION, FREE OF SPECIFIC CULTURAL
SYMBOLISM. HERE, THE STARTING POINT IS THE ORIGIN
OF LIFE EXPRESSED IN A COMMONPLACE FORM – THE EGG.

1 Look at the elements of the mandala and imagine yourself looking down onto the scene – a bird's nest with three eggs in it right in the centre of a tree's leafy canopy, with four other, surrounding nests lower down the tree.

2 Concentrate on the three eggs, first as pure shape and colour. Then lose yourself in the intricate pattern of twigs in the nest.

3 Now begin to imagine the scene as a real, three-dimensional situation. Imagine how high you are above the ground in which the tree is rooted. Imagine the sounds of birdsong all around.

4 Lastly, concentrate on the individual lives cocooned in these three eggs – the wonder of genetic inheritance, the miracle of nature's ingenuity.

As adults we may again experience birth, the cracking open of a shell, the attainment of a radical new vision.

EDUARDO CUADRA (1820–1903)

A Waterfall

THIS MANDALA SHOWS LIFE AS A POOL IN THE ENDLESS FLOW OF TIME. THERE ARE DANGERS (THE CROCODILES) BUT IF WE ARE PURE WE WILL COME TO NO HARM. BY ACCEPTING THAT WE ARE PART OF NATURE, WE GAIN SELF-UNDERSTANDING.

1 Start by looking at the source of the waters, high in the mountains. The rainbow is like a halo, symbolizing the beauty and sacredness of life when sunlight (the divine) shines through water droplets (our bodies) in the atmosphere.

2 Now think of yourself as the swimmer, free and naked in the pool. You immerse yourself fully in nature, in the way things are.

You rejoice in your being, in your incarnation within a lifetime.

3 You understand that any physical dangers are an integral part of nature too — which is why the crocodiles in the mandala appear to flow like streams themselves. Accept that the rainbow blesses the crocodiles as well as the swimmer. Life is a constantly changing balance of forces.

> *Bodies come and go like clothes.*

SRI SANKARA (C. 788–820)

Fire around the Lotus

HERE THE DEEPLY SPIRITUAL LOTUS IS SURROUNDED BY A
RING OF FIRE, SUGGESTING PURIFICATION. THIS MANDALA
ALSO SHOWS A FOUR-GATED PALACE, DENOTING SHELTER OR
SAFETY, UNIVERSAL ORDER AND THE BALANCE OF OPPOSITES.

1 Start by contemplating the outer ring of fire — a complex symbol with overtones of purification through destruction, the light of wisdom and regeneration. You are not afraid to burn off your attachments.

2 Now look at the lotus, which flowers within your mind as your spiritual vision becomes focused.

3 Lastly, take your mind into the four-gated palace at the heart of the mandala. Awakened as you are, you find the emptiness of the palace immeasurably rich and nourishing. You are at peace.

Words are only painted fire;
a look is the fire itself.

MARK TWAIN (1835–1910)

The Green Man

AN ANCIENT PAGAN SYMBOL, THE GREEN MAN IS ALSO FOUND
CARVED ON MEDIEVAL CHURCHES, A REMNANT OF MORE
PRIMAL BELIEFS. HE SYMBOLIZES THE CYCLE OF LIFE, DEATH
AND REBIRTH, AND THE GREEN SAP OF THE LIFE-FORCE.

1 Look at the face camouflaged among the greenery of foliage. Now look closer and notice that leaves are coming out of the man's mouth and flesh — he is an incarnation of nature, not merely an onlooker.

2 Recognize that in many ways we too are incarnations of nature and, conversely, that nature participates in the spirit, in the sense that natural beauty could not exist were it not for our own perception of divine harmony even in the wilderness or wildwood, far from humankind.

3 Take the mandala into your mind as an image of the unity of the cosmos and of our kinship with animals, trees and flowers.

> *Shall I not have intelligence with the earth?*
> *Am I not partly leaves and vegetable mould myself?*
>
> **HENRY DAVID THOREAU (1817–1862)**

An Octopus

1 Look at the random spirals of the octopus's eight arms. They suggest the endless energies of life as it unfolds out of the mystic centre of creation.

2 Now think of the octopus as a creature with its own brain and its own individual mental landscape — not a mind, but a kind of world-view nonetheless.

3 The octopus squirts a cloud of black ink around itself to confuse its enemies. But you are not its enemy. You co-exist with the octopus and wish it no harm. Indeed, you respect its vital essence and the validity of the life it leads. Its strange beauty is a precious aspect of your cosmos.

> *The enlightened soul is open to wonder.*
> *Every marvel of nature mirrors the miracle of being alive.*

MODERN MEDITATION FROM LISBON

Floating Lotus

THE BEAUTY OF THE LOTUS IS THAT IT REMAINS UNTOUCHED
BY EITHER THE WATER OR THE MUD THAT NOURISH IT –
SUGGESTING OUR UNDEFILED SPIRIT. THIS MANDALA HAS AN
OVERHEAD VIEWPOINT, LIKE AN AERIAL PHOTOGRAPH.

1 Look at the swirling waters of the created world – they have their own divine beauty, and so are enclosed within a flower-shaped pool surround.

2 Turn your gaze to the central, circular pool of water. As if by magic, it reflects the starry night above. This is an image of the awesome vastness of the cosmos.

3 Contemplate the lotus at the heart of the mandala, with its central yin yang symbol. The lotus denotes pure spirit, embracing the complementary opposites that exist in this world and the cosmos.

4 Lastly, let these various beauties – water, sky, stars, flower, and our own contradictory natures – harmonize in your mind and bring you peace.

Those who know the truth
are not equal to those who love the truth.

CONFUCIUS (551–479 BC)

Heart Lotus

THIS IS THE MIDDLE CHAKRA IN OUR SYSTEM OF CHAKRAS (ENERGY POINTS) WITHIN THE BODY. THE LOTUS SUGGESTS SPIRITUALITY, WHICH WE CAN FIND IN OUR HEARTS. THE CENTRAL HEXAGRAM ENCLOSES THE "SEED" SOUND, "YAM".

1 Look at the circle that frames the mandala — an image of spiritual perfection.

2 Then contemplate the leaves and petals of the lotus, which continue this symbolism. The lotus can flower within ourselves and enable us to transcend suffering. As we flower spiritually, our hearts spill out love and compassion — tender as the lotus petals, strong as the life-force itself.

3 Lastly, gaze at the central hexagram, with its intersecting triangles, representing the dualities of our existence. To open the pure heart fully we must bring into balance the complementary aspects of our life — male and female, light and shadow, mind and body, practicality and spirituality.

Heart is called the place where there is a repose in the pure light and pure consciousness.

ABHINAVAGUPTA (C. 975–1025)

Sun Lotus

THE CENTRE OF THIS MANDALA IS A SOLAR SPIRAL FROM

WHICH THE SUN'S RAYS RADIATE. THIS IS PLACED WITHIN A

LOTUS, WHICH DEPICTS BEAUTY GROWING FROM MUD JUST AS

THE SOUL RISES FROM CONFUSION TO ENLIGHTENMENT.

1 Look at the outside of the mandala, the circle, which suggests perfection. Then contemplate the lotus, a symbol of potential perfection, within that frame.

2 Now turn your attention to the heart of the mandala. The spiral here could represent the meditator's journey into the self — as well as the primal flow of energy that makes the world what it is.

3 Feel how you relate to these different elements: the perfection (outer circle) that you can find within yourself if your heart is pure; the flowering of spirituality from the soil of incarnation (lotus); the energy of the sun (spiral), which drives your earthly being.

4 Let these elements fuse together in your mind, as in the totality of the mandala. Find peaceful self-awareness in this thought.

Without self-knowledge
we are sundials in the shade.

MODERN MEDITATION FROM ROME

Nature's Harmony

CONCENTRIC CIRCLES BRING A SPIRITUAL PURITY TO THIS
MANDALA, BASED ON THE ORDER OF THE COSMOS WITH ITS
BEAUTIFUL LIFE AND EARTH FORMS. THE LOTUS DESIGN ON
THE OUTER CIRCLE EMPHASIZES THE SPIRITUAL DIMENSION.

1 Look at the sky, with its heavenly bodies, in the corners of this mandala. Then progress through the outer frame of lotus motifs. You find yourself symbolically in the realm of the mountains and the clouds.

2 Pass through the next circle into the greenery of nature, where trees, plants, birds and insects abound. This is Eden, the natural paradise.

3 Finally, penetrate to the mystic centre, which borrows from nature to express its divine creativity. Imagine the central circle as the cross-section of a shaft of light that drills into your deepest self to awaken the spirit.

All things share the same breath — the beast, the tree, the man. The air shares its spirit with all the life it supports.

CHIEF SEATTLE (1786–1866)

Cranes among Clouds

IN THE JAPANESE TRADITION CRANES ARE SYMBOLS OF
GOOD FORTUNE. CLOUDS SUGGEST THE CHANCE EVENTS
THAT TEMPORARILY CAST SHADOWS OVER OUR LIVES. THIS
MEDITATION COMBINES THESE EVOCATIVE SYMBOLS.

1 Identify the main elements of the mandala — the cranes, the blue sky, the clouds that sometimes block flying cranes from our view.

2 Keeping the mandala in your field of vision, let the details dissolve in your mind and give way to a view of empty blue sky. Let this blank sky fill your mind.

3 Visualize clouds forming a random pattern across this sky. They float across your consciousness. Then visualize a loose flock of cranes flying across the vista, passing in and out of the clouds randomly. Each crane that appears brings blessings into your life. Some of the cranes fly right through the clouds — like a happy outcome emerging from risk. Give thanks for such good fortune.

*Fortune will call
at the smiling gate.*

JAPANESE PROVERB

The Flute Player

THE FLUTE PLAYER IS AN IMAGE USED BY THE 13TH-CENTURY

PERSIAN POET RUMI TO SYMBOLIZE OUR LONGING FOR UNION

WITH THE SPIRIT. THE FLUTE YEARNS TO JOIN ITS SOURCE –

THE REEDBED FROM WHICH IT WAS ORIGINALLY CUT.

1 Look at the flute player playing at sunset. Behind him are the clumps of reeds from which the flute was cut. Imagine that the music, the flute and the player are all one, and all feeling the call of the divine.

2 Think of the flute player's music as a soundless expression of his unconscious mind – a flowering of the soul in its purity.

3 Look at the other forms of life in the mandala – the waterlilies and fishes. Think of these too as yearning for unity: all the cosmos is one.

Pure soul, how long will you travel? You are the King's falcon.
Fly back toward the Emperor's whistle!

JALIL AL-DIN RUMI (1207–1273)

Yin Yang

THE TAI CHI, OR YIN YANG, SYMBOL AT THE CENTRE OF THIS
MANDALA IS AN ANCIENT EASTERN IMAGE REPRESENTING THE
BALANCE BETWEEN OPPOSING AND COMPLEMENTARY FORCES
THAT CONSTITUTES OUR WORLD.

1 Look at the flowers and other motifs, and appreciate the contrast of the squares (the material world) with the circles (eternity).

2 Now look at the central yin yang image. See how each of the two elements contains the seed of its opposite. Relate this to the opposites balanced within you: masculine/feminine, action/stillness, insight/compassion, outward/inward, and so on.

3 Look at the smaller yin yang symbols and notice their position, between the square and the surrounding circle, touching both. Think of them as atoms that occur in everything, the universal stuff of existence.

4 See the mandala with all its embellishments as both the cosmos and the individual cell — like life itself.

> *Clay is fired to make a pot.*
> *The pot's use comes from its emptiness.*

TAO TE CHING (4TH OR 3RD CENTURY BC)

The Flower of Self

1 Visually, trace the green, wave-like shoots that surround the central flower. They are lines of energy, each a wave of becoming revealing a flower of being. The bees are in perpetual motion, their wings beating faster than the eye can see.

2 Now turn your attention to the central flower. Take its many-petalled radiance into your mind, where it rests as a still reflection of your many-petalled self, the flowering of being beyond becoming.

3 There are two bees on the petals of this flower, but you do not brush them away: you are happy to let them live their fleeting moments on the wonderful flower of the spirit — like our own lifetimes.

> *Truth is inside you.*
> *To see it you must open the inner eye.*

THE BUDDHA (C. 563–483 BC)

The Star in the Well

LOOKING DEEP INTO OUR SELVES WE SEE OUR GREATEST
RICHES – SUGGESTED BY A STAR IN A WELL. LIKE ANY STAR, IT
IS UNTOUCHABLE BUT UNDENIABLE. IT GIVES US EVERYTHING
AND NOTHING. IT IS THE OBJECT OF ALL OUR QUESTING.

1 Identify the different stages and planes of the mandala: the outer world of nature, the surround of paving, the square base within that, and lastly the hollow drop of the well itself.

2 Contemplate the star that you can see reflected in the water of the well. It shines brightly despite the darkness and the distance.

3 Think of yourself as looking right into the innermost depths of your own spirit. The deeper you penetrate, the brighter you shine. Your star is unique and beautiful, and can never be extinguished.

> *As far as we can discern, the sole purpose of human existence is to kindle a light in the darkness of mere being.*

JULIAN OF NORWICH (1342–C. 1416)

The Salmon of Knowledge

BECAUSE OF ITS AMAZING ABILITY TO CROSS OCEANS AND FIND ITS WAY UNERRINGLY TO ITS SPAWNING GROUNDS, THE CELTS ASSOCIATED THE SALMON WITH PROPHECY. MEDITATE ON THE SALMON TO COME CLOSER TO YOUR INTUITIVE WISDOM.

1 You are in the branches of a tree looking down. Two salmon are swimming in a circular pool below you. You can see also the leaves of the surrounding trees and the pool's decorative surround. Little hazelnuts are floating on the water's surface: these too are symbolic of prophetic insight.

2 Think of the salmon as a living yin yang symbol: one is male, the other female. Acknowledge both the male and female sides within yourself, as together they give you the gift of insight.

3 Draw the whole image within yourself. Feel the depths of your intuition. All reason can do is count the fish and the hazelnuts and decorate the pool edge; intuition can penetrate the inner depths, where love and truth are to be found.

Let your hook be always cast. In the pool where you least expect it, there will be fish.

OVID (43 BC–AD 17)

Jewels

GEMS WERE OBJECTS OF WONDER TO THE ANCIENTS, DIVINE
FORCES CONJURING LIGHT FROM DARK EARTH. IN EASTERN
THOUGHT, JEWELS SIGNIFIED SPIRITUAL ILLUMINATION. THIS
BEJEWELLED MANDALA CONTAINS THE YIN YANG SYMBOL, TOO.

1 Look at the different jewels and their colours. There are diamonds, denoting radiance and integrity; rubies, denoting love and courage; pearls, denoting intuition and feminine wisdom; sapphires, denoting peace and harmony.

2 See the pattern of the jewels in their delicate settings as being symbolic of the radiant and intricate order of the universe, illuminated by the intensely beautiful light of the spirit.

3 Let your eyes rest on the yin yang symbol — the creative interplay of opposites at the heart of our existence. The spirit adorns and transcends the body, as the jewels adorn and transcend male and female, light and dark, action and feeling.

> *Knowing what is enough
> is wealth.*

TAO TE CHING (4TH OR 3RD CENTURY BC)

Loving Kindness

THIS TIBET-INSPIRED MANDALA ENABLES YOU TO

SUFFUSE YOUR WHOLE MIND WITH POSITIVE FEELINGS

TOWARD OTHERS – NOT ONLY LOVED ONES AND FRIENDS,

BUT ALSO ACQUAINTANCES AND EVEN STRANGERS.

1 Imagine a loved one sitting in the mandala's centre, breathing life into the seated figure. Dwell on the qualities you admire so much in this person. Visualize him or her bathed in your love.

2 Contemplate the four symbols within the T shapes: dove (peace), hands (warmth), fire (purity) and eye (empathy). Identify all these ingredients in the quality of your love.

3 Locate family and friends in particular niches inside the mandala. Beyond are mere acquaintances and a number of strangers.

4 Welling up in the central figure and endlessly spilling outward, feel your love pouring out of you and energizing everyone. The strangers receive the same quality of love as your loved one — a love that is undiminished by distance.

*Meditate on love so that you long for
the welfare of all, even your enemies.*

THE BUDDHA (C. 563–483 BC)

Dolphins at Play

THE DOLPHIN IS PLAYFUL AND COMMUNICATIVE.
INSTINCTIVELY IT TAKES JOY IN EACH MOMENT. DOLPHIN
SYMBOLISM IS COMBINED HERE WITH IMAGERY OF THE
OCEAN, FROM WHICH ALL LIFE EVOLVED.

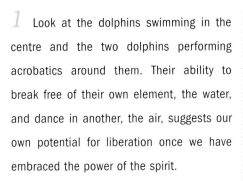

1 Look at the dolphins swimming in the centre and the two dolphins performing acrobatics around them. Their ability to break free of their own element, the water, and dance in another, the air, suggests our own potential for liberation once we have embraced the power of the spirit.

2 Contemplate the circle which the two dophins make in their dance of joy. The circle suggests both spiritual perfection and the endless cycle of life, rising and falling, coming and going, like the dolphins.

3 Think of the vastness of the ocean, and the infinite expanse of sky above it. Taking the mandala into your mind, absorb the harmony of the cosmos. Our lives are gleaming droplets of water within the shining ocean of being.

Grace is a gravity
that has learnt how to play.

MODERN MEDITATION FROM LOS ANGELES

A Water Garden

A GARDEN IS THE UNIVERSAL SYMBOL OF

HARMONY IN NATURE AND OF THE HUMAN SOUL

WHICH, JUST LIKE A GARDEN, MUST BE IN HARMONY

WITH ITSELF IN ORDER TO FIND PEACE.

1 The life-giving powers of the water, which plays endlessly through the fountain, give sustenance to the fish, just as love gives sustenance to the soul.

2 The paving around the pond is made up of uneven blocks, perfectly fitted together — a symbol of the work done by unconditional love and of love's tolerance of imperfections.

3 Notice that you cannot focus on all four of the trees that flourish outside of the garden at once, but that you can hold them at the edge of awareness, just as love can contain all things. Think of love as the soil, rain and roots of existence.

*You are an ocean of knowledge
hidden in a dew drop.*

JALIL AL-DIN RUMI (1207–1273)

Jacob's Ladder

IN GENESIS, JACOB DREAMS OF ANGELS ASCENDING AND
DESCENDING A LADDER BETWEEN HEAVEN AND EARTH. EVEN
IN OUR PHYSICAL EXISTENCE WE CAN ENJOY INTIMATIONS OF
THE DIVINE – AS LONG AS WE ARE OPEN TO LOVE.

1 Start by gazing at the earthly city. Its inhabitants are caught up in their various preoccupations. Few of the inhabitants even notice the ladder to heaven: it exists on a different scale from the mundane.

2 Now look at heaven. Its gates are within you, just as the mandala itself will be within you as soon as you absorb the whole image into your mind.

3 Look at the angels moving back and forth between heaven and earth. Their love for the divine, and the love shown by the divine to them, keeps them airborne. Think of them as messengers showing you the way.

4 Lastly, review the journey ahead, up the ladder and into the spiritual world. The angels will help you. Love provides the energy.

*Be not forgetful to entertain strangers, for thereby
some have entertained angels unawares.*

THE BIBLE, HEBREWS 13:2

Transformations

BUTTERFLIES DENOTE TRANSFORMATION – OUR AWAKENING
FROM THE DOMINANCE OF THE EGO TO A MATURE SELF-
AWARENESS. LOVE ENABLES US TO TURN OUR ENERGIES BOTH
INWARD (TO TRUTH) AND OUTWARD (TO COMPASSION).

1 Look at the butterflies in the image and choose one at random. Mentally trace its life-cycle back through the different phases: butterfly back to chrysalis, chrysalis back to caterpillar, caterpillar back to egg.

2 Now focus on the caterpillar in the centre of the mandala. Think of the potential for radical change inherent in the creature.

3 Now think of this potential for transformation in the very part of yourself that absorbs the image of the mandala. Sense your capacity for giving and receiving love in abundance, and relish the blessings that such love will bring you.

All things are complete
within ourselves.

MENCIUS (C. 390–305 BC)

A Dove of Peace

THE DOVE IS THE MOST SPIRITUAL OF BIRD SYMBOLS. IN
ADDITION TO ITS UNIVERSAL IMPORTANCE AS AN EXPRESSION
OF PEACE AND RECONCILIATION, IT CONJURES UP THE
PURIFIED SOUL — OR, IN CHRISTIAN TERMS, THE HOLY SPIRIT.

1 Within the outer circle of the mandala, which indicates perfection, contemplate the endless yet restless pattern as an image of earthly energies. Within this is a rainbow pattern, a beautiful manifestation of the life-giving spirit of the sun.

2 Now focus on the dove with its olive branch, a symbol of salvation. The dove has materialized out of pure spirit — like your own most profound qualities of love and peace. Hold the bird in your gaze as if you are seeing it through a telescope. Its background is eternity.

3 Take this dove into your mind, and relax in the knowledge that it is completely at home there. You have recognized its sign and welcome the bird and its message of peace.

Peace brings love as love brings peace.
The perfect form is the circle.

MODERN MEDITATION FROM SYDNEY, AUSTRALIA

Avalokiteshvara

THIS IS THE NAME GIVEN IN TANTRIC BUDDHISM TO THE

BODHISATTVA (ENLIGHTENED BEING) OF COMPASSION.

HE RADIATES SELF-SACRIFICING LOVE – DENYING HIMSELF

ENTRY TO NIRVANA UNTIL ALL OTHERS CAN ENTER AS WELL.

1 Any depiction of Avalokiteshvara compels our gaze and our profound admiration. Feel the energy of his goodness. It is this that enables us to accept a one-dimensional painting as a harmonious, deeply benevolent presence.

2 The *bodhisattva* sits in a lotus position on a lotus flower. Contemplate the perfection he has chosen as his setting.

3 Two of Avalokiteshvara's hands express devotion, while the other two hold a rosary and a lotus. The rosary enables him to count the repetitions of his mantra, "*Om Mani Padme Hum*," which liberates all beings from suffering. He is weightless, like an image in a mirror. He transcends all concepts – including the idea that he exists only in another dimension. Meditate and you will find him inside yourself.

*No act of kindness, however small,
is ever wasted.*

AESOP (620–560 BC)

The Dream Flag

1 Look at the colours of the flag at the centre of this mandala. Understand the blue as heaven, denoting spiritual insight, and the yellow as earth, meaning our physical world. Observe how the blue and yellow, spirit and body, are dependent on each other.

2 Now think of the blue as wisdom and the yellow as compassion — two comple-mentary aspects of spiritual self-fulfilment. Again, the interlocking design suggests how inseparable these qualities are.

3 Visualize the dream flag unifying wisdom and compassion as it undulates in the wind.

What we have to learn to do,
we learn by doing.

ARISTOTLE (384—322 BC)

The Rose of Pure Love

THIS MANDALA IS THE ROSE CROSS, A SYMBOL THAT GAVE ITS
NAME TO THE MYSTIC ORDER OF THE ROSICRUCIANS. THE
CROSS IMPLIES THE FOUR CARDINAL DIRECTIONS, WHILE THE
ROSE SUGGESTS PURE LOVE, AS WELL AS SACRIFICE.

1 Consider the cross, which incarnates the spirit in the physical world. So powerful a symbol is the cross that we can readily imagine its central point behind the rose. It gives support to the rose, whose flowering transcends it.

2 Look at all the petals of the rose, beautifying the world. Think of them as the unfolding of love within your own heart.

3 Take the mandala into your inner self, where the rose manifests selfless love, compassion and spiritual awareness.

The heart's message cannot be delivered in words.

MU-MON GENSEN (1322–1390)

Islands

NONE OF US IS AN ISLAND: WE ARE ALL JOINED TO EACH OTHER BY BRIDGES OF THE SPIRIT. THIS MANDALA TRANSLATES THIS UNIVERSAL METAPHOR INTO A REPRESENTATION OF THE JOURNEY FROM THE SELF TO OTHER PEOPLE.

1 The starting point is the earthly city. Think of its millions of individuals, all with their unique lives and circumstances, dreams and worries. All are strangers to you.

2 Now think of an archipelago of desert islands. Each has people stranded on it, refugees from the overcrowded city. They stand at different ends of their islands, unable to connect with each other.

3 In your mind, set out on a voyage to each island in turn to bring its inhabitants together in neighbourly love through the power of your own love for all humankind.

4 Finally, take the whole mandala into your heart. See the islanders smiling at each other rather than looking out to sea.

The only way to have a friend is to be one.

RALPH WALDO EMERSON (1803–1882)

A Snowflake

THE SNOWFLAKE IS FLEETINGLY BEAUTIFUL: WE SCARCELY

HAVE TIME TO ADMIRE IT BEFORE IT MELTS. SUCH IS THE WAY

OF THE WORLD: OUR LIVES, OUR LOVES, ARE ENDLESS

CHANGE. BUT AT THE CENTRE IS THE UNCHANGING SPIRIT.

1 Look at the snowflake in this mandala, one of an infinite number of snowflakes, yet complete and perfect within itself. Observe its perfect symmetry, and be aware as you appreciate the design that no other snowflake in the entire cosmos is identical to this one. Let this thought sink into your mind. Spend a few minutes relishing this frequent miracle.

2 Consider the snowflake's intrinsic strength, which comes from its unique beauty. The snowflake is fleeting yet flawless.

3 Imagine that the snowflake is on the point of melting. You are observing it in the moment of its being, from the fleeting viewpoint of your own lifetime.

Weak overcomes strong,
soft overcomes hard.

TAO TE CHING (4TH OR 3RD CENTURY BC)

Sailing the Storm

STORMY SEAS HAVE TESTED THE FORTITUDE OF MANY A
SAILOR. THIS MANDALA SHOWS A SHIP IN PERIL. USE IT TO
FIND YOUR OWN RESERVES OF COURAGE, AND AS A SPIRITUAL
COMPASS WITH WHICH TO PLOT A SAFE COURSE.

1 You are looking down on a sailing ship from a bird's-eye view. You are safe, dry and calm but the ship is in trouble — buffeted by gigantic waves, sails threatened by lightning, torrential rain lashing down on the crew.

2 Now scan the mandala as a whole, and notice its harmony. Appreciate that a world where ships can be lost to violent storms is still a beautiful world, and that even in extreme danger you have the resources of spirit to give you strength.

3 Look at the four compasses in the mandala — your tools to steer by. Perhaps these are love, faith, acceptance and compassion.

4 Now look again at the mandala as a whole. See it as reflecting life's totality, with all its challenges and contradictions.

Only that which cannot be lost
in a shipwreck is yours.

AL-GHAZZALI (1058–1111)

A Samurai Sword

THE SWORD IS A SYMBOL OF AUTHORITY AND DECISIVENESS.
THIS MANDALA SHOWS A SWORD GUARD SURROUNDED BY FOUR
SWORDS AND THEIR SCABBARDS. MEDITATE ON IT WHEN
PREPARING FOR A LIFE CHANGE OR A BOLD DECISION.

1 Look at the central circle, and within that the decorative cross — an image of creation within spiritual perfection

2 Now look at the swords and scabbards. They indicate the decision itself. Use them, if you wish, to check that your resolve is firm. To do this, think of the four pairs of swords and scabbards as a progressive scale, ranging through possibly, probably, certainly, inevitably. Can you move through this scale without hestitation?

3 Lastly, make your decision to act in the way that you believe is right. Focus your will on moving through the centre of the mandala. The flowing embellishments around the centre suggest right action, in accordance with natural law.

*Confusions and dangers
are nothing but the mind.*

DOGEN (1200–1253)

Eternal Feminine

THIS MANDALA ENCLOSES FEMININE SPIRITUALITY WITHIN

THE PROTECTIVE WALLS OF STRENGTH AND COMMON SENSE.

AT ITS CENTRE IS THE YONI, THE FEMALE CREATIVE SYMBOL,

HELD LOVINGLY WITHIN THE LOTUS OF ENLIGHTENMENT.

1 Look at the square enclosure with its double-buttressed walls. It is deeply set within the spiritual — the outer circle and the lotus, both of which suggest purity. The square is the foundation that grounds us and prevents us from losing touch with the eternal truth.

2 Enter the lotus and let the lotus enter you. Meditating upon this mandala, you absorb all the energies and essences of the eternal creative feminine principle, which brings us into the physical world and at the same time gives us the gift of intuitive wisdom.

For a woman is the everlasting field
in which the self is born.

THE MAHABHARATA (C. 400 BC–AD 200)

The Holy Grail

FOR AN ARTHURIAN KNIGHT THE HOLY GRAIL MEANT SELF-
KNOWLEDGE, REDEMPTION, IMMORTALITY. HERE THE GRAIL
IS AT THE CENTRE OF THE ROUND TABLE, SURROUNDED BY
THE HELMETS OF THE KING AND SIX OF HIS KNIGHTS.

1 Look at the sword in the stone, which only the future king can remove. True meditation pulls the sword from the stone, as the physical world becomes subordinate to the spiritual.

2 Recognize that the king is a symbol of yourself. The knights around you are your personal qualities. See yourself as inwardly protected by armour and magic shields.

3 Lastly, feel worthy to approach the Grail, which is at the same time empty yet full of love. Imagine yourself holding the Grail and feeling its transforming power.

I searched for God and found only myself.
I searched for myself and found only God.

SUFI PROVERB

Confronting the Minotaur

THE MINOTAUR, A BULL-LIKE CREATURE THAT LIVED IN A
LABYRINTH ON THE ISLAND OF CRETE, STANDS FOR ALL OUR
INNER DEMONS — ATTACHMENTS, FEARS, FAILINGS IN LOVE.
THROUGH MEDITATION WE CAN TAME THE MONSTER.

1 Think of the Minotaur as a source of negative energy that you need to defeat. As you enter the maze you unroll a red thread from a spool: this is your connection with the world of safety, your knowledge that the Minotaur can never really harm you.

2 Trace your way through the confusion of many turnings — you are moving deeper and deeper into the depths of your being.

3 When at last you reach the centre, you find that the Minotaur is already harmless. What took courage initially was facing the truth about yourself.

4 Now take the mandala into your mind — maze, thread, bull and all. Dwell upon it as the image of your spiritual heroism.

*It is not because things are difficult that we do not dare,
it is because we do not dare that they are difficult.*

SENECA (C. 4 BC–AD 65)

Celtic Dragons

THE FIRE-BREATHING DRAGON IS FEARFUL AND POWERFUL,

BUT IN THIS MANDALA THE DRAGON'S POWER IS POURED

INTO THE ENDLESS KNOT OF SPIRITUAL PERFECTION.

EARTH AND SPIRIT BLEND IN COSMIC HARMONY.

1 Look at the fire that issues from the four dragons' heads at the top and bottom of the mandala. This is the physical energy of nature, which can become transmuted into spiritual energy. The fire forms a circle — its spiritual character is endless.

2 Now rest your eyes on the dragons' bodies transformed by spirit into an endless knot of eternal perfection. Matter passes into spirit, which purifies it and enfolds it within an all-embracing cosmic harmony — giving birth to the "pearl of great price" in the mandala's centre.

3 Let the mandala become the centre of your awareness and allow the opposites of matter and spirit to blend together, to manifest the wholeness that is our essential nature.

Accept whatever happens
and let your spirit move freely.

CHUANG TZU (C. 369–286 BC)

A Stained-glass Window

THE BEAUTY OF STAINED GLASS IS A GIFT OF SUNLIGHT —

ITS IMAGES, LIKE OURSELVES, WOULD BE LIFELESS WITHOUT

THE SUN. THIS MANDALA EVOKES THE PEACE OF A CHURCH

OR TEMPLE AND REJOICES IN THE SUN'S RADIANCE.

1 See the trefoils and quatrefoils of the design as symbolic of nature — the universe of infinite forms. The subject of the window is the harmony of the natural world, shown by leaves, flowers and bunches of berries.

2 Now start to see the pure design taking form as an actual window which you are observing from inside a sacred building. Appreciate its artistry and workmanship.

3 Lastly, imagine that the window is lit from behind by bright sunlight. All the colours glow beautifully. The window has become a perfect symbol of nature animated by spirit and, at the same time, of human creativity animated by spiritual wisdom. As you draw the mandala deep into your mind, recognize that it reflects the essence of your true self.

*Truth and morning
become light with time.*

ETHIOPIAN PROVERB

Time and the Universe

THINKING ABOUT THE NATURE OF TIME CAN PRODUCE
CONFUSION, EVEN DESPAIR. FORGETTING THE CLOCK AND
SEEING TIME AS THE ETERNAL FLOW OF THE UNIVERSE
IS A REASSURING AND REFRESHING VISUAL MEDITATION.

1 Identify the elements of the mandala: time as a flow, the river changeless yet endlessly changing; the seasons; the movements of stars, Earth, Sun and Moon; the four symbols of butterfly (briefer life than ours), tree (longer life), spiral (infinite time) and Möbius strip (infinite space).

2 Still holding the mandala in your field of view, imagine all the separate meanings of these different aspects of time dissolving into the great river, the flow of the cosmos.

3 Feel yourself entering the great river of time, interfusing with its flow: the river is within you and you are within the river. The mandala is a drop of water, one of an infinite number of such drops. Relax into the endlessness of time and space.

*Every instant of time
is a pinprick of eternity.*

MARCUS AURELIUS (120–180)

Dragon Energy

THE DRAGON IS THE PARADOX OF BEING – LIGHT AND DARK,

CREATION AND DESTRUCTION, MALE AND FEMALE, AND THE

UNIFYING FORCE OF THESE OPPOSITES. THE DRAGON'S FIRE

IS THE PRIMAL ENERGY OF THE PHYSICAL WORLD.

1 Look at the mandala's seven-headed dragon and imagine its overwhelming, invincible power. Trace this power in the ring of flames. Nothing more awesome can be imagined in all the universe.

2 The seven heads symbolize the mystical number of the cosmos. They are the sum of the number of divinity (three) and the number of humankind (four).

3 Finally concentrate on the knot of dragons' necks at the centre of the mandala. This is where all contradictions are resolved.

*The phantasmal is the
bridge to the real.*

SUFI SAYING

Sri Yantra

THIS IS A SIMPLIFIED VERSION OF THE SACRED HINDU SRI
YANTRA. THE SRI YANTRA'S PATTERN OF INTERLINKING
TRIANGLES HAS A COMPELLING MYSTIC BEAUTY,
REPRESENTING THE TIMELESS CREATIVITY OF THE UNIVERSE.

1 Focus on the centre of the mandala and its opposing sets of triangles — these represent the male and female principles which in their fusion give rise to creation.

2 Now turn your attention to the geometry surrounding the image. Consider the equal-armed cross, whose elements represent the created cosmos, and the circle, denoting spiritual perfection.

3 Contemplate the central point of the Sri Yantra, which is called the *bindu*. This is the source of all creation. And your own mind, as it absorbs this yantra into itself, is unfolding like everything else in the cosmos, past, present and future, from this transcendental, creative source.

*We meditate upon that divine sun, the true light
of the shining ones. May it illuminate our minds.*

THE GAYATRI VERSE OF THE VEDAS (C. 5000 BC)

The World's Weather

THE WEATHER IS A SYMBOL OF ENDLESS CHANGE. IT OFFERS A
LESSON IN ACCEPTANCE: IF WE FIND IT DIFFICULT TO ACCEPT
THE WEATHER REGARDLESS OF ANY PLANS WE HAVE MADE,
WE HAVE A LONG WAY TO GO IN OUR SPIRITUAL JOURNEY.

1 Look at the sun, which is shown in each of the four corners of this mandala. It is always there, driving life's energies, even when obscured by cloud. In the same way, our identity and our spirit are unaltered by shifts of fortune.

2 Now concentrate on the mandala's depiction of clouds, rain, rainbows, snow and rough seas. All this weather belongs to one vast self-regulating global system, which the mandala as a whole symbolizes.

3 Lastly, focus on the central point of the mandala — the still source of the endless streams of energy that bring all weathers and all other changes into the cosmos. This is the energy from which we are made. Take the mandala deep into your mind where that energy finds its still centre.

Love is the wind, the tide,
the waves, the sunshine.

HENRY DAVID THOREAU (1817–1862)

Cause and Effect

IT IS SAID THAT WHEN A BUTTERFLY FLAPS ITS WINGS IN JAPAN,
IT CAUSES A HURRICANE IN LOUISIANA. TO SEE THAT ALL THE
WORLD'S EVENTS ARE CONNECTED IS TO UNDERSTAND THAT
WE SHOULD ALL TAKE RESPONSIBILITY FOR OUR ACTIONS.

1 Look at the three interconnected gear wheels. They are an obvious form of cause and effect.

2 Now look at the butterfly, whose wings flap metaphorically to create a storm on the other side of the world. This is cause producing effects invisibly. Such unseen connections occur throughout existence.

3 Focus on the mandala as a whole: its asymmetrical form around an inner wheel conceals the harmony of the cosmos. In the same way, any imbalances in our own lives conceal the unified whole of the spirit.

4 Finally, contemplate the hub of the central wheel. Take it deep into your consciousness and become aware that all life revolves around a still central point.

> *Through what is near,*
> *one understands what is far away.*

HSUN-TZU (C. 300–238 BC)

The Endless Knot

WELL KNOWN AS A CELTIC SYMBOL, BUT WITH PARALLELS IN HINDU, BUDDHIST AND CHINESE TRADITIONS, THE ENDLESS KNOT REPRESENTS INFINITY, THE ENDLESS FLOW OF TIME AND MOVEMENT, AND THE JOURNEY OF THE PILGRIM.

1 Become aware of the endless knot in the mandala — the elaborately interlaced thread without a starting point. See this as a transcendental state beyond the material world. Visually trace the thread to satisfy yourself that it has no end.

2 Focus on the central cross within the circle — a symbol of the physical (the cross) fused with the spiritual (the circle).

3 Now let these two images — the encircled cross and the endless knot — enter your mind as a single expression of the eternal truth of existence: all existence is time-bound, but ultimately it rests timelessly within the divine or eternal spirit. Relax in this timelessness throughout your meditation.

The end and the beginning of being are unknown. We see only the form in between. So what cause is there for grief?

THE BHAGAVAD GITA (C. 500 BC)

Arches of the Heavens

THE DOME OF A TEMPLE OR CHURCH IS OFTEN MANDALA-
LIKE WHEN SEEN FROM BELOW — A PATTERN MADE UP OF THE
ARCHES OF WINDOWS AND CRISS-CROSSING ROOF SUPPORTS.
THE RESULTING VIEW, OF COURSE, IS HEAVENWARD.

1 Pick out the main features of the mandala — the view directly upward into an elaborate dome. The three-dimensional geometry is complex, but don't try to decipher each decorative or structural element, just absorb the basic architecture, and the four decorative flower motifs.

2 Think of sunlight passing through the windows of the dome and bringing it to life, in the same way that sunlight gives life to living beings.

3 Think of the image as a two-dimensional pattern again, and take it deep into your mind. Your mind is now contemplating the heavens and the life-affirming light of divinity. You are peacefully at prayer — although you are asking for nothing.

> *Geometry is an abstraction of beauty.*
> *Add light and this beauty becomes spiritual.*

MODERN MEDITATION FROM SAN FRANCISCO

A Pagoda

THE PAGODA ADDS A SPIRITUAL DIMENSION TO THE JAPANESE GARDEN, DEPICTING OUR ASCENT TO HEAVENLY BLISS THROUGH STAGES OF ENLIGHTENMENT. THIS MANDALA ALSO SYMBOLIZES BALANCE BETWEEN NATURE AND ARTIFICE.

1 View the pagoda as a succession of separate temples, one built on top of another. This is the triumph of art over formlessness, yet its purpose is not to aggrandize humanity but to assert the vitality of the spirit.

2 Notice that the pagoda has open sides. The building is a meeting-point of emptiness and solidity.

3 Contemplate the uppermost level, with its pointed roof. This symbolizes spirit — the crowning glory of the created world. Whatever stage you are at on your journey, you can see your destination clearly. All the ladders on which you will climb are already present and there for the finding.

Logic will get you from A to B. Imagination will take you everywhere.

ALBERT EINSTEIN (1879–1955)

The 51 World Tree

WITH ITS ROOTS AROUND THE EARTH AND ITS BRANCHES IN
THE HEAVENS, THE WORLD TREE SYMBOLIZES OUR ABILITY TO
TRANSCEND OUR HUMBLE ORIGINS IN THE DENSE REALM OF
MATTER AND ASCEND TO HEAVENLY BLISS.

1 Contemplate the world tree, so vast that its canopy stretches over day and night. The tree's fruits are the good things given to us by the divine — the harvest of virtues, including love, compassion, peace and self-awareness. In your knowledge of this tree, and of its fruits, you are immensely privileged. You are aware that, as long as you keep this knowledge in your heart, you will be fulfilling your true destiny.

2 Sense the essence of the world tree rising through the trunk and branches as you bring them deep into your mind, and through the channels of your heart and spirit. This vital essence is both material and spiritual.

3 Understand that if a branch falls to the ground, the tree still stands. In the same way your spiritual essence is eternal, whatever accidents befall your body.

When the wind of pure thought rustles among its leaves,
the World Tree whispers the name of the divine.

MODERN MEDITATION FROM GERMANY

Palace of the Gods

TRADITIONAL MANDALAS WERE OFTEN SEEN AS DIAGRAMS
OF THE PALACE OF THE GODS. THIS MODERN VERSION SHOWS
A PLAN OF THE PALACE AND SIDE-ON VIEWS OF EIGHT
PAVILIONS. THE PALACE IS BOTH THE COSMOS AND THE SELF.

1 In your mind enter the sacred palace gardens, as defined by the outer circle of the mandala. Here you are outside time and space. The large circle and the smaller ones inside it generate a spiritual atmosphere.

2 Think of the four pavilions in the outer wall of the palace as the domain of earth, air, fire and water. All four elements dwell in the mandala, in the cosmos and in your own self. The fifth element, ether or spirit, has its own inner enclosure. Enter the inner square now. Once inside, you are able to transcend earthly barriers (the concentric square walls) and bathe in the sacred fountain.

3 The fountain flows inside you endlessly, the life-force that sustains your being. It is blessed by the divine, and brings infinite peace to your spirit.

*God is consciousness that pervades the entire universe
of the living and the non-living.*

SRI RAMAKRISHNA (1836–1886)

Further Reading

The following is a brief guide to books on meditation
and mandalas.

Bucknell, R. and Kang, C. (ed.) *The Meditative Way*.
RoutledgeCurzon, Richmond (UK), 1997.

Coogan, M. D. (ed.) *World Religions*. Oxford University Press,
New York, 1998; Duncan Baird Publishers, London, 1998.

Eastcott, M. J. *Silent Path*. Rider, London, 1969; new
edition Rider, London, 1989.

Fontana, D. *The Meditator's Handbook*. Element Books,
Shaftesbury (UK) and Boston, 1992; new edition Thorsons
Publishers, London, 2002.

Fontana, D. *Learn to Meditate: The Art of Tranquillity,
Self-Awareness and Insight*. Duncan Baird Publishers,
London, 1998; Chronicle Books, San Francisco, 1999.

Fontana, D. *Meditation Week by Week*. Element Books,
Boston, 2004; Duncan Baird Publishers, London, 2004.

Gawain, S. *Creative Visualization*. Bantam Books,
New York, 1982.

Goleman, D. *The Meditative Mind: The Varieties of
Meditative Experience*. Aquarian Press, Wellingborough
(UK), 1989; Jeremy P Tarcher, Los Angeles, 1996.

Govinda, A. *Creative Meditation and Multidimensional
Consciousness*. Quest Books, Wheaton (Illinois), 1976;
Unwin, London, 1977.

Hanson, V. (ed.) *Approaches to Meditation*. Quest Books,
Wheaton (Illinois), 1973.

LeShan, L. *How to Meditate*. Turnstone, London 1983;
Little, Brown & Co., New York, 1999.

McDonald, K. *How to Meditate: A Practical Guide*. Wisdom
Publications, New York, 1995.

Naranjo, C. and Ornstein, R. E. *On the Psychology of
Meditation*. Viking Press, New York, 1971; Allen & Unwin,
London, 1973.

Smart, N. *Dimensions of the Sacred: An Anatomy of the
World's Beliefs*. HarperCollins, London and New York, 1996.

Steinbrecher, E. C. *The Inner Guide Meditation*. Weiser
Books, London and New York, 1987.

Tucci, G. *The Theory and Practice of the Mandala*.
Rider, London, 1969; new edition Dover Publications,
New York, 2001.

Wallace, B. A. et al. *The Bridge of Quiescence*. Open Court
Publishing Company, Chicago and La Salle (Illinois), 1998.

Wood, E. *Concentration: An Approach to Meditation*. Quest
Books, Wheaton (Illinois), 1967.

General Index

For ease of reference, this index has been divided into two parts: the first is an index to concepts that occur throughout the book; the second is an index of specific symbols.

Entries in *italic* type refer to captions to photographs. Entries in **bold** type indicate symbols that are included in the title of the mandala.

A
acceptance 23, 24
analytical mind, letting
    go of the 25, 26
artistic spirit 25

B
bindu 40, 143
bodhisattva 114
breathing 14, 48
Buddhism 10, 12, 34, 47,
    114, 149 *see also*
    Tibetan Buddhism

C
calming the mind *see*
    stillness
cause and effect **147**
Celts 56, 61, 98, **135**, 149
chakras 83
Chartres cathedral,
    France 12, 65
Chinese traditions 149
Christianity 11, 28–9,
    65, 113
colours, symbolism of
    12, 47, 116
cosmic consciousness 42
cosmos 40–43

D
distractions, resisting
    see stillness
Dogen 49
dream **116**

E
Eastern traditions 9, 11,
    92 *see also* Chinese
    traditions, Japanese
    traditions
elements 31–2, 54, 62, 157
    fifth element (spirit)
    54, 62, 157
enlightenment 34, 56,
    68, 153
expert guidance/teachers
    17, 27, 29
eyes, stilling movement
    of 15, 19, 20,
    21, 43

F
feminine **129**
focus 14, 19 *see also* eyes,
    stilling movement of

G
geometrical shapes 11, 17

H
Hinduism 10, 12, 62,
    143, 149

I
Islam 11

J
Jainism 12, 20
Japanese traditions
    89, 153

Judaism 62
Jung, Carl 43, 46,
    47–8, 50

K
kindness 35–7, **103**

L
letting go 35, 45
love 37–9, **103**, **118**

M
mandala(s)
    as a friend 18, 28, 50
    as a mirror 33
    becoming one with a
        27
    choosing a 16–18, 29,
        35, 38
    definition of 9, 10,
        25, 26
    in architecture 11,
        12, 17, 65, 76, 137,
        150, 153
    in ourselves 32
    making a 43–5, 50
    purpose of a 28
    Sanskrit meaning of 10
    traditions 11–12
mantras 15, 114
meaning, the search for
    23, 25, 46
meditation
    benefits of 15
    clothing for 49

definition of 14,
    28–9, 33, 49
how long to practise
    20, 49
how to practise 19, 32
mandalas and 9, 10,
    14–16, 19, 21, 24,
    25–6, 27, 29,
    36–7, 40–42, 50
starting 16, 19
when to practise 49
where to practise 19,
    32–3, 49

N
Native Americans 59
nature **87**
    mandalas in 18, 30–33
    oneness with 32–3

P
pagan symbol 76
peace **113**
perseverance 50
psychotherapy 43, 50
pyramids (of Egypt) 17
Pythagoras 17

R
relaxation 15, 26
Rosicrucians 11, 118
Rumi 90

S
"sacred geometry" 17, 30

seeing, the art of 23, 24
self 32–5, 46, 94
self-discovery 15, 33
selflessness 68
stillness 14, 15, 20, 26,
    43, 49
Stonehenge 17
symbols/symbolism 9,
    10, 46–8
symmetry **67**

T
Tibetan Buddhism 12,
    16, 18, 68, **103**, 116
time **138**
transformation **110**

U
universe 42, **138**
    see also cosmos
using this book 18, 50, 53

V
vision, the power of 16,
    22, 27

W
Western traditions 11

Y
yantra 10 *see also* Sri Yantra
    in Index to Symbols

Z
Zen tradition 28, 49, 50

Index to Symbols

A
angels 109
arches **150**
Avalokiteshvara **114**

B
bees 94
birds *see individual entries:*
    cranes, dove,
    Thunderbird
bird's nest **71**
butterfly 110, 138, 147

C
Celtic Cross 11, 17, **54**
circle(s) 9, 10, 47, 54,
    67, 83, 84, 87, 92,
    105, 113, 135, 143,
    149, 157
city 109, 121
clouds **89**, 144
compass 125
cranes **89**
crocodiles 72
cross 47, **54**, 118, 143,
    149 *see also* Celtic
    Cross, "rosy cross"

D
dolphins **105**
dome 11, 150
dove 103, **113**
dragon(s) **135**, **141**

E
Earth 39, 138
eggs 71
endless knot 135, **149**
eye 103

F
fire **74**, 103, 135, 141
fish 90, 107 *see also*
    salmon
flag **116**
flower(s) 92, **94**, 150
    see also individual
    entries: lotus, rose,
    waterlily
flute player **90**
foliage *see* greenery
fountain 157

G
garden **107**, 157
gods **157**
greenery 76, 87
Green Man **76**

H
hands 103
hazelnuts 98
heart 39
heavens **150**
hexagram **62**, 83
Holy Grail **130**

I
islands **121**

J
Jacob's ladder **108**
jewels **101**

K
king 130
knights 130
knot 141 *see also*
    endless knot

L
labyrinth *see* maze
ladder **109**
lotus 12, 68, **74**, **81**, **83**,
    84, 87, 114, 129

M
maze **65**, 132
Minotaur **132**
Möbius strip 138
Moon 138
mountains 87

O
ocean 105
octopus **78**
olive branch 113

P
pagoda **153**

palace 74, **157**
paving 107
pearl 135
pilgrim **65**

R
rain 144
rainbow 72, 144
river 138
rose 39, **118**
"rosy cross" 11, 118

S
salmon **98**
scallop shells 39
seas 145 *see also* ocean
,seasons 138
ship 125
sky 87, 89, 105
snow 144
snowflake **122**
spiral(s) **56**, 59, 78,
    84, 138
square 47, 68, 92, 96,
    129, 157
Sri Yantra 40, 67, **143**
stained-glass window **137**
star(s) 81, **96**, 138
Star of David 62
storm **125**, 147
sun 39, 56, 61, **84**,
    138, 144
sunlight 72

swimmer 72
sword **126**

T
Tai Chi *see* yin yang
tears 67
thread 132, 149
Thunderbird **59**
tree 71, 98, 107, 138
    see also World Tree
triangle 32, 40, 47,
    62, 67, 83, 143
triskeles **61**

W
water 81, 96, **107** *see also*
    fountain, ocean,
    seas, waterfall
waterfall **72**
waterlily 90
weather **144** *see also* storm
well **96**
wheel 147 *see also* Wheel
    of Truth
Wheel of Truth **68**
World Tree **155**

Y
yin yang 68, 81, **92**, 101
yoni (female creative
    symbol) 129

Picture Credits

The publisher would like to thank the following people, museums, and photographic libraries for permission to reproduce their material. Every care has been taken to trace copyright holders.

However, if we have omitted anyone we apologize and will, if informed, make corrections to any future edition. **Page 8** Getty Images, London/Charles Krebs; **13** British Museum,

London; **31** OSF/Photolibrary.com/William Gray; **41** British Museum, London; **51** Getty Images, London/Peter Samuels